PRAISE FOR
WOMEN OVERCOMING O-SYNDROME

"Having been the only woman in the room for so many years, in so many companies, over the course of my career, it is my greatest hope that this book will provide guidance and strength to all women leaders. I will be sharing it with the amazing women in my network so that they will know they are not alone."

— Kelly Lockwood Primus
Senior Vice President, Leading Women, LLC

"What a gift Theresa gives us—the telling of shared experiences from wise and courageous sisters. So many women will recognize themselves in these pages. It's from healing our most painful memories that we blossom into true self-actualized women. The only antidote to O-Syndrome is to be O-mnipotent! Now is our time to rise to our unlimited power! Thank you, Theresa for being the catalyst!"

— Shary Hauer
Founder of The Hauer Group, Executive Advisory and Coaching Firm, and Author of Insatiable: A Memoir of Love Addiction

"I strongly believe that you can't wait for an invitation to have a seat at the table. It will never come. You just have to pull up a chair and sit down."

— Mayerland Harris
Group Vice President, H-E-B Houston Food and Drug, Central Market and Joe V's Smart Shop

"Theresa tells it like it is - every woman will relate to O-Syndrome. Get ready to see yourself and your friends, mom, sisters, and colleagues in her stories. Thank you, Theresa, for writing a book that is so authentic and revealing about our experiences."

— Joan Toth
Senior Consultant, Diversity & Inclusion, Simpactful and Advisory Board Member, Gender Fair

"Theresa and collabHERators have written an excellent must read for women everywhere! You will be inspired!"

— Harriet Harty
Chief Human Resources Officer, Allstate

"*Women Overcoming O-Syndrome* is a must read for every woman in corporate America. Dealing with the frustration of being overlooked in the workplace despite my many years of experience and education is tough. In this book, Theresa shows women how to step into the limelight and excel in their career."

— Sasha Nelson
Medical Assistant, Nemours Children's Hospital

"As I've maneuvered through the information technology field, I've encountered many 'good old boy' networks of men who discriminate at all levels. Through personal examples, Theresa exposes these behaviors. I found myself relating to the indignities. Yet, Theresa left me with an optimistic view for taking charge and overcoming my unfounded feelings of inadequacy."

— Catherine Mackel
IT Specialist, Federal Government

"Can women get to the top like men? You bet we can. But let's face it, the climb is steeper and the juggling act that much harder. If you ever wonder if you've got what it takes to last the distance toward whatever ambitions inspires you, this book is for you. Packed with relatable stories and wise insights, it will help you bring your bravest self to your biggest challenges. Daily."

— *Margie Warrell*
Women's Leadership Coach, Speaker and Best-selling Author of Stop Playing Safe

"Congratulations, and well done, Theresa and collabHERators for reminding women (me) how amazing we are!

— *Vanessa Womack*
Principal, Vanessa Womack Consulting

Women Overcoming O-Syndrome

Also by Author

O-Syndrome: When Work is 24/7 and You're Not

Women Overcoming O-Syndrome

Real, Raw, Unapologetic

THERESA M. ROBINSON
and CollabHERators™

Master Trainer TMR & Associates, LLC

Women Overcoming O-Syndrome™ Copyright © 2018
Master Trainer TMR & Associates, LLC

All rights reserved. No part of this book may be reproduced by any mechanical, photographic, or electronic process, or in the form of phonographic recording; nor may it be stored in a retrieval system, transmitted, or otherwise copied for public or private use without the prior written permission of the publisher.

Master Trainer TMR & Associates, LLC
Houston, TX
info@MasterTrainerTMR.com

Theresa M. Robinson, primary author

ISBN 978-0-9988420-2-8 Paperback
ISBN 978-0-9988420-3-5 eBook

First Edition

This is a work of nonfiction. Some names and identifying details have been changed.

Dedication

To my circle of family and friends whose love and support inspire me to keep going.

To all women. I see you. I hear you.

Table of Contents

Foreword	i
Acknowledgements	vii
Introduction	1

PART I: What We Face

Chapter 1: Talked OVER	23
Chapter 2: OVERtalked	39
Chapter 3: OVERlooked	61
Chapter 4: OVERjudged	77
Chapter 5: Passed OVER	117

PART II: What We Do to Ourselves

Chapter 6: OVERachieve	133
Chapter 7: OVERcommit	161
Chapter 8: OVERaccommodate	179
Chapter 9: OVER Isolate	193

PART III: What We Want from Allies

Chapter 10: Not Every Woman Has Your Back	213
Chapter 11: Not Every Man Is Clueless and Actionless	237
Conclusion	269

Foreword
Becky A. Davis and Jeffery Tobias Halter

Prior to January 10, 2018, I didn't know Theresa. And I wasn't accustomed to getting messages on LinkedIn like the one I received from her that day. She introduced herself and relayed that she had just read a *Houston Chronicle* newspaper article about me *that same day*, that she had just downloaded my book from Amazon *that same day*, and that she had just registered for my January 25 Bosspreneur® breakfast in Atlanta *that same day*.

"Wow!" is what I wrote in my message back to her. I love it when people take immediate action, and that's exactly what Theresa did. It still takes me by surprise to hear that something I've said or done has impacted someone from far away.

Sure enough, two weeks later in Atlanta, in a meeting room within The Coca-Cola Company headquarters, among many women business owners, there she was, seated at one of the tables, front and center, having flown in from Houston to attend. Somehow, I never doubted that she would show up. Meeting her in person was a complete pleasure. She walked up to me and said, "I'm the one who contacted you from Houston about the article." I immediately remembered her. Her energy was contagious, and I felt like I was connecting with a long-lost friend.

Months later, when Theresa asked me to write the main foreword and shared the details of the project with me, I was so intrigued by her description and characterization of O-Syndrome that I said "yes" without hesitation. I don't accept all invitations, but I knew this book would help change women's lives. I immediately connected with it. Having spent twenty years in corporate before leaving to start my own business, I can tell you that what you'll read in this book has been my journey as well. I have lived all the chapters of this book.

While working in corporate America, in a male-dominated field, I was quite often the only African American female leader. There were times when I was overlooked and had to step out to be seen. I've been overjudged because of my confidence in my skills. It pushed me to overachieve to be accepted. I've overaccommodated to make people feel good while being miserable. I had a tendency to overcommit, because I didn't want to hurt anyone's feelings or let anyone down, even when I was already overextended with enough on my plate. I was miserable trying to stay ahead of the game. It took some years to "wake up" and understand that I needed to take care of me first. I accepted that I was enough. It's not easy, but it's a worthwhile journey. Now I live unapologetically.

Like Theresa, I believe in women sharing our stories, helping, and supporting each other, and learning from each other. This belief is what led me to create the Bosspreneur® Business Circle for women entrepreneurs and for women in corporate who want to feel valued and get paid what we're worth. It doesn't have to be hard for all of us to access the help we need. When we come together as women, we are powerful and unstoppable. For the last six years, I have attended Black Enterprise Women of Power Summit because it's a place that creates an environment of acceptance, connection, and friendliness while learning how to navigate our lives and careers as women. I believe that every woman should have a place to go that celebrates women's successes. This book is also that place.

More than a book, it's *our* book. And it contains so much of what strengthens what I call Boss Girl Magic—

connections, strategies, advice, belonging, support, accountability, and more. Boss Girl Magic happens when we take action toward our dreams and watch them manifest no matter what treatment we encounter or obstacles we face. Boss Girl Magic happens when we fight our fear in the process—together. As with this book, Boss Girl Magic is real, raw, unapologetic. With *Women Overcoming O-Syndrome*, we're reminded that we are not alone and that our voices are more powerful than we know. Reading the refreshingly down-to-earth and, at times, laugh-out-loud funny stories is like sitting down with best friends and having honest conversation.

Becky A. Davis is the founder, CEO and chief bosspreneur® of MVPWork, LLC, a consulting firm that helps thousands of women entrepreneurs to develop their business and accelerate business growth. The national spokesperson for The Coca-Cola Company's 5by20 women entrepreneur initiative, Becky is also the founder of the Bosspreneur Business Circle, a member network committed to advancing women entrepreneurs. A leading business expert, business growth architect, speaker, and coach, Becky has authored eight books including, *40-Days of Prayer for My Business, It's Okay to be Great* and *Boss Moves: Think Big, Go Hard to Live Better*.

* * *

What does a self-proclaimed "old, white guy" and this author share in common? And why am I writing a foreword for her book for women? To put it simply, I care. Theresa and I are both passionate about advancing women in the workplace, and we are committed to gender equity.

I first met Theresa at a corporate leadership event ten years ago when she was leading the training. I was immediately taken with her passion and unbridled enthusiasm. She was the type of person who was not just doing training, but was committed to driving long-term positive change.

We continued to cross paths a few more times due to our connection with Network of Executive Women (NEW). Hearing her speak to NEW audiences, I was struck by her ability to build instant rapport and connect with women by being authentic regarding her own experiences—the good, the bad, the ugly. To use Theresa's description, she is a catalyst who can "get people to talk about their stuff and then call them on their stuff without pissing them off." So, when she explained her book and project to me, I was immediately honored to be asked and all-in to support this important work. I knew that if anybody could pull off getting real, raw, and unapologetic stories of women, Theresa would! And she has!

This must-read book, written by and for women, is vitally important. Especially now when the world needs to hear a lot more of the voices that have been silenced and muffled. In my work as a corporate gender strategist, I work to help companies leverage and advance women through active male engagement. You see, men and women are having vastly different experiences in the workplace—and it's an imperative that we create conversations about these differences in order to create real and sustainable change.

Theresa's dual focus of looking at what women face from external challenges and what women face from their own internal struggles provides a sometimes unexpected, but always welcomed honesty. For any woman who has been hesitant to share her voice, I say, be encouraged, be inspired by the pages that follow.

This book is also a must-read for men. Men need to hear women voice their experiences, so they can be moved into action to be real allies and advocates. Women have the power to make this book required reading for men. Put it in the hands of your partner, your son, your brother. Talk about it together. Use the end-of-chapter questions to initiate a conversation with a male coworker.

The stories in this book revolve around topics that men often don't want to talk about and are powerful enough to keep the conversation going. My personal favorite is chapter 11, "Not Every Man Is Clueless and Action-less." I love that this chapter provides a balanced perspective on what some men are doing right, while pointing out what more men can be doing. One of the ten end-of-chapter strategies directed at men is the Male Advocacy Profile quiz found on my website (http://ywomen.biz/male-advocacy-profile/), where answering twenty short questions will reveal where a man is on the Male Ally Continuum.

As the father of a daughter and also a new grandfather of a granddaughter, I have a responsibility to advocate for women in the workplace and engage other men in the process. If we don't do this work today, then by default our daughters will face the same bias, male-dominated work environments, and gender pay issues that currently exist. These conditions do not reflect current values and must be changed. Together we can create a brighter future for our daughters—and all women.

Jeffery Tobias Halter is the president of YWomen, a strategic consulting company focused on engaging men in women's leadership advancement. Founder of the Father of Daughter Initiative and creator of the *Gender Conversation QuickStarters* Newsletter, Jeffery is the country's leading male expert on advancing women and engaging men. Speaker, consultant, and thought leader, he has authored two books, *WHY WOMEN, The Leadership Imperative to Advancing Women and Engaging Men* and *Selling to Men, Selling to Women.*

Acknowledgments

My deepest gratitude to

my Source, through Whom all things are possible;

an amazing tribe of CollabHERators for graciously sharing not just their voices, but all of themselves;

Mark Robinson, my book project manager, a role that does not do him justice, for lending his keen eye for design and layout;

Brenda Heald, my developmental editor, for being a collabHERator from the very beginning with *O-Syndrome: When Work is 24/7 and You're Not*;

Shannon Gettins, for serving as my secret weapon;

Dr. Jo Lichten, dietitian and friend, for sharing her knowledge.

Women Overcoming
O-Syndrome

Introduction

"Well-behaved women seldom make history."
— Laurel Thatcher Ulrich

1973.
John Love Elementary School.
Jacksonville, Florida.

His name was Leroy. *Yes, that's his real name.* At the time, I had another name for him, which wasn't appropriate for a seven-year-old. You see, Leroy was my tormentor for weeks until the unthinkable happened.

Theresa M. Robinson

I was in second grade, and that school year was the first time I had a male teacher. I found Mr. Lawson to be a bit of an oddity, not because he had orange hair, with a matching mustache and beard, but because he was a man. My previous teachers for kindergarten and first grade had both been women, and I just assumed all my teachers would be female.

On the first day of school, he arranged us in assigned seating. Vertical rows. For more than thirty kids, there were five rows. Mr. Lawson's process for assigning seats was not to organize us alphabetically, or by who had the best-looking book bag—which I thought made more sense—but to sort us in boy-girl-boy-girl fashion. That's how I ended up seated between a rock and a hard place, aka Eric and Leroy.

Leroy occupied the seat immediately behind me and announced that he'd be trouble by gleefully commenting, "Ha-ha. I get to sit by you." And not in a "good, let's be friends" kind of way. More of an "I'm going to make your life a living hell" kind of way.

As a young girl, I often wore my hair in two pigtails or ponytails. My hair was long, and so my ponytails extended past my shoulders. Based on how my mother styled them, they hung more so down my back. It wasn't long before Leroy determined that it would be fun for him to yank on my ponytails whenever he felt the urge. The first time he did it during quiet reading time, my knee-jerk reaction was to turn around and face him.

"Stop," I hissed.

What that got me was a stern look from Mr. Lawson and a snicker from Leroy.

This went on for days with me thinking that I would just deal with it on my own. When I finally decided to enlist the help of Mr. Lawson, his response told me he didn't think it warranted his intervention.

"He means no harm. That's his way of letting you know that he likes you. Sometimes boys do that. Just ignore him, and he'll soon get bored and stop."

If this is how boys show girls they like them, then what the heck is marriage going to be like? And how am I supposed to ignore him yanking on my ponytails when I'm trying to do my work?

I wanted to scream at him. "But Mr. Lawson, he pulls my hair...a lot."

"Well, have you thought about wearing your hair differently, so he doesn't have anything to pull? He'll get the message."

What?! Are you kidding me?! That's your solution?! You're supposed to be the smart grown-up, and that's your solution?! What's a clearer message than "stop" issued by a teacher?

The message that my seven-year-old brain couldn't fully process back then was that Mr. Lawson believed that I should be the one to adjust and adapt. It was my fault for wearing my hair in a style that provoked Leroy.

Perhaps I should just wear a paper bag over my head, so Leroy can truly focus on his school work.

In my naïveté, I took Mr. Lawson's advice to heart.

But as it turned out, he was wrong.

For a week after his advice, I wore my hair in a pinned-up, secure bun at the top of my head, a request I had made of my mom without providing her a reason, and about which she didn't say a word. I still maintained that I could handle Leroy without getting her involved.

The last thing I wanted was my mom visiting the school. If you remember ever living with the fear of embarrassment that your mother would come to your school to get to the bottom of something, then you'll understand it when I say that her visit would not have ended well for anyone involved. Especially for me. As a single parent of three girls, my mom had been clear to us about speaking up and standing up for ourselves. If she had known about Leroy, she would have demanded from me why I had let it get this far.

Leroy must not have liked my new hair style as it had deprived him of his hair-yanking ritual. Without my hair to pull, he had resorted to light thumps on the back of my neck.

"Quit it."

Thump. Thump.

"I said quit it."

It was like a sick dance, and he was enjoying every minute of it.

What would be Mr. Lawson's advice now if I asked? Keep myself covered with a turtle-neck during August in Florida?

One day on the playground as I was talking with friends, out of the corner of my eye, I saw Leroy heading toward me. He looked possessed. Like he had had too many pixie sticks at lunch or something and needed to let off some excess energy. As he got closer, I could see the determination in his wild eyes.

He picked up speed and started running toward me yelling, "I'm gonna getcha, Theresa!"

His buddies were over in the corner, and they were laughing and cheering him on.

Oh no! He's coming for me!

Out of sheer panic, I took off running. My friends just stood there in shock watching as Leroy chased me across the playground and onto the blacktop.

My anger was bubbling up to the surface. Anger at Leroy for habitually tormenting me. Anger at Mr. Lawson for not doing anything about it. Anger at myself for running and not dealing with this once and for all. I mustered up all my adrenaline-induced outrage, and while running, turned around and screamed at the top of my lungs.

"STOOOPPP!"

Leroy froze.

And so did my feet. But the rest of me kept flying forward. I fell over, landing on a concrete ridge, smashing my chin, and splitting it open, resulting in emergency transport to the hospital for stitches. The permanent scar, I still carry today.

I recall Mr. Lawson picking me up from that cold, concrete slab to carry me inside while I continued to scream, soaking his white shirt with blood.

I stared up at his crazy, orange beard and heard him muttering.

"I'm sorry. I'm so sorry."

I had paid for that apology with my blood.

More pressing in my thoughts, however, was Leroy himself. I remember thinking that despite the hole in my chin, I had won. He would surely never bother me again.

And he never did. For the remaining three years of elementary school, he never did.

I later discovered that he had told his friends that he'd stopped bothering me because "she's crazy."

Perhaps this is where it starts. Perhaps this is why men can be "so good" at discounting women and rationalizing their own behaviors. *She's a liar. She's loose. She's crazy.* They've likely had plenty of practice since boyhood. Leroy was never held accountable for his actions that led ultimately to my fall. Technically my fall was an accident. It didn't matter that I was being chased. I tripped and fell while running on the playground. However, to keep intact his "reputation" and "standing" with his peers, Leroy created a narrative that relied on slandering me.

Crazy! Imagine that!

Crazy brave is more accurate. On that playground that day, there was so much at stake for a girl being chased by a boy and not knowing his endgame. And so, not knowing his intent, but carrying the context of prior interactions, I was brave enough to turn and scream out a four-letter word that had immediate power once I put the force of my whole being behind it.

My previous "stops" had been hissed whispers. My "quit its" had been low mutters. I had been the one embarrassed by the unwanted attention and on some level, I felt both ashamed and responsible.

After all these years, forty-five to be exact, my scar hasn't completely faded. Today, I proudly bear it on my chin. It's visible to others when I hold my head high and serves as a reminder for me to turn and face challenges head-on no matter how big and scary they might seem. When I hang my head low, the scar disappears as do my courage and fighting spirit. Despair and defeat are much heavier to bear.

As evidence of our wounds, scars are sometimes on the outside for others to see. Other scars are on the inside that others can't readily see. Every collabHERator within these pages bears scars. Reminders of what we've endured and overcome, our scars dare to defy what others may deem ugly and damaged. We've paid the high cost of our scars and have persevered to now recount our stories to others.

I've embraced my scar and the power its story represents. I and the women in these pages have made conscious decisions to reclaim and control our own narratives and to draw strength from our experiences no matter how scarred, harassed, or wronged we've been.

I learned several valuable lessons that day on the playground, one of which is that my voice is indeed powerful, but I must first believe that it's powerful. Sound will always pierce silence. Voiced will always trump the unvoiced.

The Ban on "No" Lifted (and That There Was Even a Ban in the First Place!)

As I write this introduction, a major story has hit the news. Maybe it flew under the radar for some, but for those who pay attention, it carries with it far-reaching implications. As reported by CNN on February 13, 2018, Kaneysville Elementary School in Ogden, Utah, holds an annual sixth-grade dance on Valentine's Day, intended to promote inclusion and kindness. According to school tradition, students are instructed by their teachers to say "yes" when a classmate asks them to dance.

This year, however, parents were not having it. No doubt influenced by the current shift in the gender conversation and angered by the audacity of the school, parents were quick to launch an all-out social media protest against the school's tradition. Specifically, girls were getting the message that they have to say "yes." And boys were getting the message that girls can't say "no."

It appears the school also got the parents' message. The school district quickly released a statement, effective immediately, that the instructions for the dance will be different moving forward. All students will be free to say "no."

Where to even begin? It's the Leroy effect all over again. As the expression goes: "Same shit. Different day."

From an early age, girls (and boys) receive gender messages that get constantly reinforced such that by the time a woman reaches the workplace, certain behaviors and expectations are imbedded. That girls are expected to adapt and adjust is an especially damaging paradigm. Particularly, that girls are expected to be agreeable and say "yes" has already had far-reaching implications in the realm of sexual assault.

At the age of seven, I was advised by an authority figure to change my hairstyle so that Leroy would **not act badly**. The girls at Kaneysville Elementary School were instructed by authority figures to say "yes" and not say "no" to boys' dance invitations so that the boys would **not feel badly**. And it was a message that the boys were aware of, which makes it even more dangerous.

That's a lot of pressure to put on girls at any age, being made to feel responsible for another person's actions and feelings without any regard for our own preferences and feelings.

And consider the false sense of entitlement being fostered in the boys.

Today, I'll ask for a dance that she can't refuse.
Tomorrow, I'll demand [fill in the blank].
See where this is going?

O-Syndrome in Context

Do any of us even remember when we first experienced gender-biased treatment? Sometimes it was subtle. Sometimes it was blatant. Some of us may have been too young and lacked life experience to recognize it and call it for what it was because we'd become so conditioned that it was normal. The best we could hope for was to try and navigate it and not let it be a blocker.

When women arrived in the workplace in droves during the 1960s, the seeds had already been planted as to how we would be received and treated by a patriarchal system that was vested in the status quo. We joined male-dominant work teams, many of which went through the motions to welcome us, but their words and actions quickly betrayed check-the-box pretenses of welcome.

Fast forward to 2018. Women's and men's lives, both inside and outside of the workplace, have grown busy. In fact, incredibly busy. The busyness and its effects are the reason for my first book, *O-Syndrome: When Work is 24/7 and You're Not*. I coined the term O-Syndrome, because, having served as a corporate facilitator for more than twenty-five years, I noticed the sheer number of professionals self-reporting being incredibly overstressed, overwhelmed, overcommitted, and overloaded. Many had fallen into the O-Syndrome habit, largely due to the tremendous pressure at work to perform and achieve.

As I conducted research and compiled my notes for that initial book, I was intrigued by the clear pattern emerging that underscored what I had been hearing many years prior from women with whom I'd worked. Women were citing gender issues as a major source for their overstressed and overwhelmed state. Specifically, women were pointing to the impact of gender bias and gender inequity both inside and outside of the workplace. (And adding to this, women of color were contextualizing the intersection of gender and race within their experiences.)

Where We Stand Today

Though I didn't fully realize it, the foundation was already being laid for this follow-up book to address women's unique experiences with O-Syndrome. (My entire career journey is also a part of that foundation.) While working on that first book, it grew obvious that this book had been pursuing me. In my conversations with women, what we had experienced and were experiencing continued to dominate the ways in which we talked about and characterized O-Syndrome. It was evident early on that the subject of gender was much more prominent for women and demanded an expanded treatment: how are women's experiences with O-Syndrome informed by their shared experiences with systemic gender bias and discrimination?

Over the years, I've been privy to the experiences and perspectives of hundreds of women. I didn't find them. They found me. We found each other. As a facilitator/speaker interacting with audiences all over the world, I am naturally drawn to women and their experiences. Once I issued the formal call about this project, the responses were immediate. Accomplished, professional women were eager to talk more about what they've experienced and what they've learned. They detailed the costs of being female in male-dominated environments.

Why should you care about their experiences and what they have to say? Because of their titles? No. (I rarely include that.) Because of their industries? No. (I rarely include that either.) Because they were gracious and generous enough to set aside an entire day to be interviewed or because they wrote and submitted their stories? No. You should care because they embody the voices of our grandmothers, our mothers, our sisters, and our best friends. What they have to say transcends title and industry, and spans across time and place.

There has been much time with not much difference separating my John Love Elementary school's Leroy experience from Kaneysville Elementary school's dance rules. Different time. Same timing. *Our thinking is conditioned while we're young.* Different place. Same placement. *Our thinking is conditioned when we're under school authority.* While it's important to celebrate the progress we've made in gender equality, if we don't address what's still broken, we forfeit our chance to fix it and are bound to keep repeating it.

I've devoted my career to helping others be their authentic, whole self in all areas of their lives. What women are experiencing threatens that. This book was voiced into existence because it's time to unite and widen the conversation such that our experiences are validated. It's time to work collectively for change.

Once this project grew and took on a life of its own, I knew that it was not mine alone. Specifically, during the face-to-face interviews, through the questioning, the listening, the aha moments, the insights, the lessons learned, the raucous laughter, the frustrations, and yes, even the tears, I couldn't help but think about how empowered we each are when we have a voice. How empowered we are when we rise up from the shadows of misplaced expectations, imposed invisibility, and unfair treatment to say out loud what needs to be said. This book is our say.

Think about how much more empowered we become when our voice joins up with another voice that joins up with yet another voice. The #MeToo and #TimesUp movements have clearly illustrated what collective voices can do, while the #MentorHer initiative shows what advocates and champions can do.

Free to De-FINE Yourself

For some of us who have stayed quiet out of habit, when others ask, "How are you?" let's think twice about whether a response of "fine" accurately captures our reality, especially if what we're presently experiencing is not fine. *He interrupted and talked over me. My manager cautioned me about being aggressive. I'm burned out.* This book is our permission to declare that things are not always fine. Let it serve as our rallying cry to give voice to our hurt, our frustration, and our outrage at the gender inequities that continue to plague our community, our workplace, and our world. When our voices are silenced and stay silent, and we bear our challenges alone, we miss out on our great power.

Stand up.
Speak up.
Act up.
Join us.

I feel like it's not just me.
I feel relieved.
I feel fired up.
I feel validated.
I feel like I can take a deep breath.
I feel a part of an amazing tribe of women who are in this with me.

Get Real

I consider myself a feminist. I know that. Here's where I struggle. On one side, being a feminist means that I have to respect that all women can make their own choices. But then I also struggle with women who make certain choices and hold certain ideas that are harmful. If a woman's opinion makes little girls think they need not be equal or

> can't be equal and that they need to be submissive, that's harmful.
> — Katerina, a collabHERator

Just as the end of the Holocaust, the abolition of slavery, or the women's rights movement could never shift *all* minds and change *all* attitudes, rejecting old gender paradigms requires constant rejecting, re-educating, reframing. It is still believed, perpetuated, and embedded in minds and in cultural and organizational systems that the way to be a successful woman is to be agreeable and don't make waves; smile, be present, but not a presence; be seen, but not heard; wait to be recognized; bury and suppress what you really think and feel; take care of and nurture others even to the detriment of self.

That was then. This is now. As we get closer to the end of 2018, what is behind us is not as important as what lies in front of us. Imagine if each of us purposefully ended and began the year with our voice. That would be fine!

How Women Experience O-Syndrome

What women face is a continuation of the phenomenon I call O-Syndrome: being talked over, overtalked, overlooked, overjudged, and passed over. At the same time, there is yet another side of O-Syndrome that women do to ourselves when we overachieve, overcommit, overaccommodate, and over isolate.

> **Get Real**
> I'll just say that I'm so relieved O-Syndrome has nothing to do with orgasm, LOL! Because haven't we women already suffered enough?! You probably won't even

> include this in the book, but we have to laugh about some things in order to not cry about all things.
> — Pat, a collabHERator

O-SYNDROME CHECKLIST

How many of these aspects of O-Syndrome have you experienced in the past year?

- Talked over: to be interrupted, especially in meetings, while you're in the middle of talking, usually by a man, who often may go on to repeat exactly what you've just said and get the credit for it
- Overtalked: to be dismissed verbally (i.e., "mansplaining") in a way that is patronizing and demeaning because the offender assumes you lack knowledge
- Overlooked: to be looked past or not be taken notice of as if you're invisible or as if your input or voice is not valued
- Overjudged: to be unfairly assessed via gender stereotypes or assumptions on grounds other than data and facts
- Passed over: to be looked past or disregarded, often in favor of a man, for a job, assignment, or promotion without fair consideration for your experience, qualifications, or potential

> **Get Real**
> I speak up to both men and women. I'm like my grandmother, who reached a point where she didn't give a damn. She spoke her mind to whomever. She had no

> hesitation about saying exactly what she felt and exactly what she thought.
> — Kim, a collabHERator

With how many of these aspects of O-Syndrome have you struggled in the past year?

- Overachieve: not only to strive for success above and beyond the standard or expected level, often at the detriment to yourself and your relationships, but also to feel compelled to do so due to feelings of unrelenting, self-imposed pressure
- Overcommit: to excessively obligate yourself beyond your ability or capacity to fulfill, often to please others or to prove and re-prove yourself to others
- Overaccommodate: to obsessively provide services or favors and make adjustments, whether requested of you or not, for the convenience and comfort of others, even at the inconvenience or expense of yourself, oftentimes accompanied by overapologizing
- Over isolate: to deliberately or inadvertently separate and insulate yourself from the help and support of others due to the faulty thinking that a strong and successful woman with help and support may be perceived as incapable

Get Real
Over it! Single mum of two teen-aged boys, with a full-time job in a struggling, private company. The only daughter in a sea of male siblings. Uber-mum six days a week and trying to undo the effects of poor male role-

> modeling! Sounds like the perfect recipe for overwork, overtaxed, overdrive and overwhelm. And it is!
>
> — Jane, a collabHERator

A Word about Real, Raw, Unapologetic

This book is a collection of my own personal experiences as well as the experiences of women from different industries, from various career stages, and from diverse demographics, whom I call collabHERators, and without whom this book would not exist. Assuming different names of their creative choosing, collabHERators in these pages range in age from twenty plus to sixty plus, from black to white, from admin to C-suite, from atheist to believer, from heterosexual to lesbian, from single to widowed. From the diversity and myriad of voices, what unites us is our shared challenges with O-Syndrome.

> **Get Real**
> You have my permission to quote and use my name. I'm too seasoned (old, experienced to hide - LOL) and let it all hang out! Trying to pass on any wisdom. I will become a caretaker for my mother again who has recently been diagnosed with stage one breast cancer, at 83. She is a leukemia survivor, five years. So, not too busy to help others as directed, as long as there is joy and life left in me.
>
> — Vanessa, a collabHERator

From my collabHERators, I insisted on genuine, unpolished, what's-really-going-on accounts and what-you-really-think-and-feel sentiments. So if authenticity of voice is what you crave, look no further. Other than editing for ease of readability, I have endeavored to carefully preserve the stories, voices, and words.

The stories invite and engage freedom in the sense that releasing our voices is cathartic and freeing. Each woman was encouraged to just say it like it is and how she feels it—the good, the bad, and the ugly—without apology. So, in the spirit of full disclosure, I ask you, reader, to please refrain from judgment.

Warning. Sentiments are often crass and not veiled in political correctness, tactfulness, civility, or etiquette. If you're easily offended or blush at the mere suggestion of an off-color thought or remark, then this is not the book for you. If you're quick to claim "male-bashing" or discrimination, move on. (The former is admittedly harsh, while the latter is illegal.) If any of this applies to you, stop reading now and pursue an alternative selection that doesn't announce itself with real, raw, and unapologetic content. Please find a selection more suitable to your tastes and sensibilities.

How This Book Is Organized

This book is divided into three parts. Part I focuses on the external O-Syndrome forces that women face. Within it are five chapters, each addressing a particular O-Syndrome aspect (see the checklist, p.14): talked over, overtalked, overlooked, overjudged, and passed over.

Part II focuses on the internal O-Syndrome forces to which women subject ourselves. Within it are four chapters, each also addressing a particular O-Syndrome aspect: overachieve, overcommit, overaccommodate, and over isolate.

Part III focuses on what women want from allies and contains two chapters. One chapter focuses on the status and importance of woman-to-woman support, and one focuses on the need for more man-to-woman support.

But identifying aspects of O-Syndrome is only part of it. Each chapter also contains concrete strategies and tactics designed to take you out of O-Syndrome mode and move you forward into overcomer mode.

Chapter elements include the following:
- Opening quotes
- Real, raw, unapologetic stories, anecdotes, and interview excerpts
- "Get Real" moments that capture distinct collabHERator voices and previously pent-up emotions
- "Get Over It!" strategies that address the chapter's O-Syndrome focus, most of which can be implemented right away
- Reflection questions that set the stage for the "Do-Over" and "Make-Over" challenges, but can also be used to guide journaling or to guide facilitating group discussions
- "Do-Over" challenges that rely on hindsight wisdom applied to past events through actions designed to build a new foundation for future actions
- "Make-Over" challenges that plant the seeds of transformation with short-term or long-term self-empowering actions with big impact

What I Hope This Book Will Mean to Us

This book is both part of a movement and an environment within which women have shared stories related to personal experiences connected to our identity as women. I hope that you'll closely connect with at least one woman from this book and bond over your shared experience or sentiment. As women, even if the specifics of our stories are different, in many ways we're all on the same journey.

The rollercoaster of emotions that leap from these pages includes weariness, bemusement, frustration, feistiness, anger and more. Our tears are tempered with hope and resolve. What ultimately rises to the top are the fierceness and determination born of our fighting spirit. I pay tribute to women all over the world who make the decision to get up every morning and put one foot in front of the other to do what is good and right and noble despite all the crap.

This book is our safe space to share, to vent, to laugh, to cry—and to provide strategies that help, support, and empower us in the face of gender inequity. And I hope it will unleash in us what others, and even we, have managed to relegate to below the surface. We're not the overreactive, emotionally inferior gender that we've been portrayed as. We are uniquely multifaceted. We want to have our say about the injustice of how we continue to be regarded and treated. Within these pages be comforted and supported by many women who share in this journey. Find an increased sense of peace, more wisdom in our choices, more courage to speak up and act up. It's time to shatter paradigms and bust up more stereotypes.

As you read, please know that your voice matters.
It has always mattered.
It will always matter.
Always.

> **Get Real**
> It's not just about women realizing we have voices. It's about others shutting up long enough to recognize that women have voices!
> — Jackie, a collabHERator

Are you ready to get real? Let's get started.

Oh, wait. One more very important thing.

I don't have everything all figured out.

And collabHERators don't have everything all figured out, either.

The message we don't hear enough of is that NO ONE has everything all figured out.

But, maybe, if we connect our wisdom with somebody else's wisdom and then connect that wisdom to more wisdom, and so on and so on, we'll finally figure things out—together.

PART I

What We Face

"Yes, we've '...come a long way, baby.' We've gained hard-earned seats at the table. The issue remains. It's still <u>his</u> table."

— Theresa M. Robinson

Chapter 1

Talked OVER

"Don't mistake politeness for lack of strength."
— Sonya Sotomayor

"One of the issues I kept saying to my students is you have to learn to interrupt. When you raise your hand at a meeting, by the time they get to you, the point is not germane. So, the bottom line is active listening. If you are going to interrupt, you look for opportunities...Women have to be active listeners and interrupters—but when you interrupt, you have to know what you are talking about."
— Madeleine Albright

"Even in a culture where people are well meaning, there are sometimes 'microaggressions.' People who just cut you off. You'll be talking, and someone will interrupt you. That's become a big pet peeve of mine."
— Susan Wojcicki

Only ten minutes of class remaining. And there it was. Right on schedule. The overwhelming feeling of dread and anxiety that washed over me at this same time every week. The feeling had grown so regular that I could set my watch by it.

"Theresa, can you give us the female perspective?"

Ugh. There it is. I wanted to say, "No, but it looks as though I'm capable of giving you the 'only person with a brain' perspective." Professor McMillan had no idea how especially insensitive this question was within the context of a graduate seminar course comprised of four male students and me. I guess I should be somewhat relieved that he never once asked for the black perspective since my presence in the class checked that box also.

"No, I can't."

"Alright then. For next week, read..."

Really?! Clueless. Absolutely clueless. I guess I had been subjected solely to the male perspective for the past 110 minutes.

The Shakespeare seminar in which I had enrolled was during my first semester as a graduate student in a doctoral program at Cornell University. It was one of the worst experiences of my graduate career. Right up there with the time I downed too many NoDoz pills studying and then called my ex-boyfriend fifteen times. I regret them both equally.

The Shakespeare seminar was the only class I ever took in which I was the only female in the room. I was reminded of it ad nauseam. I had grown frustrated early on in the course when explaining to Professor McMillan and my classmates that the limited representation of my gender in the class did not make me the voice of all women. It just made me mad.

Do they really not understand that it doesn't get any clearer than that? Perhaps I should borrow from Shakespeare: "Lord, what fools these...[men] be!"

Plus, often during class when I had attempted to add my thoughts to the discussion, I had been quickly cut off and talked over by one or more of my classmates. As if to model to the class that this was acceptable behavior, Professor McMillan would often cut me off and talk over me as well. The talking over me had also evolved into walking over me. Having grown weary and resentful, I had long since checked out. I never again enrolled in one of his courses.

> **Get Real**
> Boys are conditioned to constantly tell each other how great they are and may interrupt others to do it. Girls are conditioned to be polite and respectful and wait our turn so as to let the other person finish their point. When you bring that conditioning into the workplace, it gets very uncomfortable. Women wait for their moment that may never come. And even when our moment comes, we may not be heard because our voice is lower, or we're not really seen. Or they don't get our meaning because they consciously or unconsciously ignore it or can't understand it. Many times, when I say something and then later somebody else makes the same comment, I make it a point to say, "Well, I said that already." Sometimes they get all flustered and try to back track.
> — Whitney, a collabHERator

Outclassed by Gender

Looking back, *if* I were to be generous, I suspect Professor McMillan thought he was extending to me a great kindness in giving me the last few minutes of class to speak.

But I'm tired of being the generous one that helps to make excuses for others' treatment of me.

I am calling out the fact that for nearly two hours every week for sixteen weeks of my life, this man fostered and encouraged a gender-hostile academic environment! Why would he even need to devote the last few minutes to me if I had been included in the discussion in the first place? I will never get those sixteen weeks back. The few minutes he saved at the end of each class felt like obligatory crumbs at a feast offered by the host to someone at the table made to feel she didn't belong there. It was humiliating, demeaning, and degrading. I didn't want crumbs. I deserved more than crumbs.

Grading the Cost

It's hard to know sometimes what recourses to avail ourselves of when there is a power dynamic in place. As a first-year female graduate student with an issue against a highly regarded, respected, male, tenured professor, I didn't feel like I would be taken seriously. It didn't matter if it was a serious bias issue. Would my fellowship funding be in jeopardy? How might my reputation be affected? How many questions would I have to answer? Would I be ostracized? I might be summarily dismissed and labeled too sensitive about Professor McMillan's "genuine attempts" to solicit my participation. In the end, I determined that silence, though not preferred, was safer.

It's that inner dialogue that talks us out of what we know feels wrong and helps to perpetuate the cycle. By the time women enter the workforce, we've been subjected to multiple gender inequities and offenses about which we've often had to make decisions, and we've also been mentally conditioned. To somewhat quote Shakespeare again, what we face can be a matter of making constant decisions regarding whether "to be [one who speaks up] or not to be [one who speaks up]."

And based on each instance of unfair treatment, verbal or otherwise, imagine the inner turmoil. Imagine if each of us during our lifetime spoke up about and reported each gender offense to which we've been subjected. How high do you think the number might be? What if we just consider one day in our own life, especially because many of us can make pretty good educated guesses due to the ongoing patterns in our own environments.

Cast as "other," I learned what to expect in that graduate seminar, and I managed to, albeit not thrive, but survive the entire semester. With a final grade of an A-, I had barely scraped by. An A- is not commendable in grad school. I don't know if it's different now at Cornell, but grad students were assessed on their academic performance with either an A+, A, or A-. Any other grades were akin to failure.

My A- put me at the bottom of the class, a final grade Professor McMillan had the power to determine. He also had the power to change the culture in his classroom. He didn't. Leaders who themselves remain entrenched in their thinking and behavior cannot possibly fundamentally change the culture because culture flows from the values of those with power, influence, and authority.

Even though my written papers were well received, my lack of participation in the class did me in. That would be *his* assessment. That was also likely my male classmates' assessment. My assessment differs. My A-, rather than the "W" that would have appeared on my transcript if I had withdrawn from the class, is a symbol of my endurance. I kept returning to that class week after week for sixteen weeks despite my treatment. I was developing my armor.

The unfortunate and yet fortuitous result of this experience and other experiences like it is that, whether what happens to us is perceived fair or not, many women get really good at being resilient. It's something I've been hearing over and over again from collabHERators. Because many of us in our own way have arrived at a realization that certain behaviors may not change anytime soon, we develop tough outer skins and unleash a harsh, badass inner dialogue that is self-protecting and self-insulating. With it, we fight back.

Whereas Professor McMillan and the other students in the room heard me say the words "I can't," I never whispered or stuttered, and I never cowered or crouched in my physical stance. If they heard it correctly the way I intended, I was declaring a defiant "I won't." I was able to keep attending that class week after week because my rebellious thoughts kept me going. Mental warfare is what prevented me from being utterly defeated and broken.

I refuse to give you the satisfaction.
I'm smart enough to be here.
I refuse to be put on display.
You don't deserve to benefit from what I think.
Your loss.
What a bunch of jackasses!

Is it Manners or Communication Styles?

> ### Get Real
> I've found myself in these situations where I've had to violate what I, for the most part, consider rude. I've had to violate that by jumping in and talking over people myself. Here's how I justify it. "If I don't get in there now and talk over you in order to make my point, I'm not going to be able to at all. There's not going to be a space for me

> based on the way this meeting is going." It feels so unnatural when I do it, but I do it when I feel I have no choice.
> — Bethany, a collabHERator

Bethany, who was raised by parents who instilled in her the importance of good manners, certainly struck a chord with other collabHERators with whom I spoke who feel forced to justify something that doesn't feel natural or comfortable in order to enter a male-dominated arena. We go through a process. We first assess the meeting and how it's going. Based on it being like a free-for-all where people are overtalking and talking over others, we muster our courage and come out swinging. Many describe it as a fight or battle because that's what we feel like—that it's a battle to have our voices heard and seriously regarded in certain environments.

> **Get Real**
> Some days I say and do nothing and let it happen. I'm not passive and cowardly. I'm saving my strength to win the war and not stir up a battle. Call it strategic wisdom.
> — Gail, a collabHERator

The burden for the adjustments is on women to take on behaviors that may feel unnatural or uncomfortable in order to compete. And then these same behaviors are the ones for which we are often condemned.

> **Get Real**
> When I was growing up, manners meant something. Conference calls at my company are sanctioned anti-manners events. All these people talking over other

> people. Most of the talking is by men. And most of the interrupting is by men. It's so hard to insert yourself. It's horrible. I hate it.
>
> — Heather, a collabHERator

Learning from the Peacock

"I have a picture of a peacock I keep on my desk. In the image, the peacock has its feathers extended outward. When I'm on conference calls I look at the peacock, and I hate these people. They're all peacocks. They want to puff themselves up and show their tail feathers. I just keep looking at the peacock while they're not letting me speak. My anger was enough to get me to jump in and start talking over them. Now I'm famous for it."

That's how Yvonne, a cancer survivor and mother of two, explained how she went from being talked over to being the one doing the talking over. "After so many times, my anger continued to grow. The anger took me through stages. It propelled me to trade in my silence. I still get angry that I have to talk over people to be heard, but it's better than being angry and also not heard. I had this determination that I would not be bested by a group of peacocks."

"My advice to other women is to find your inner source of strength, focus on it, and channel it outward to speak and act on your own behalf. For me, it was the image of conquering the peacock. Be prepared though for what reactions you may get."

"My boss, who is a woman, commented during a conversation with me that I have done well with some difficult situations. To everyone else though, she comments in jest that I'm not nice anymore. When I feel forced to insert myself and do it enough times, people understand I have something to say and have a voice. I believe it's the quieter voices that usually have the most to say, but others miss out on it because they're so busy talking."

"It's troubling that when some of us find our voice and talk over others in order to be heard, we're considered not nice or bitches. Talking over others is a last resort for me; it's not my natural state. Men have always talked over others, but there is not that same general negative association. The hard part we're all still trying to figure out is how to navigate this without being perceived on the extreme of either too nice or bitchy. Men have never had to navigate this space the way that women do."

When We Don't Know

Have you ever not known something, but rather than admit it you attempted to bullshit your way through it? A male friend of mine told me that men do this all the time, and that it's expected in certain situations. Many collabHERators were sure that this contributes to the ease with which men freely talk over and overtalk others.

CollabHERators also theorized that on the occasions when women bullshit, we feel badly about it. The alternative for us though is equally as bad. Either bullshit our way through or stay silent and be perceived as incapable or worse. What should we say when we flat out don't know what to say? What do we do when we don't know what to do? Maybe we have some data and we've done our homework, but we just come up blank.

There are times when I flat out, unequivocally just don't know. I also know the pressure in some situations where my silence may be perceived as ignorance and also an indictment against all women or all black people, especially if I am the only woman in the room or the only person of color in the room.

I am learning how to be okay with not knowing and how to pronounce my "I don't know" with confidence. I've discovered that when I let go of the need for certainty and perfection, both closely related to the overachiever gene, it can be quite freeing. Not knowing leaves room to sometimes live in the questioning for a while.

> **Get Real**
> I get so preoccupied with making sure I gather my thoughts perfectly in my head before I'm willing to speak up. Often though, I miss my chance and the moment passes. The conversation has turned to a new topic. And then it starts all over again. All these brilliant thoughts in my head never get expressed out loud. And everyone regards me as silent for the entire meeting.
> — Jean, a collabHERator

Shamed into Silence

What do Senator Elizabeth Warren and Stormy Daniels have in common? It almost sounds like the opening to a tasteless joke. If only it were just a joke. What ties these women together is how a power dynamic or power structure plays a pivotal role in silencing and shaming them. They are both condemned when they speak up to or speak out against what or who is powerful and prominent.

"She was warned. She was given an explanation. Nevertheless, she persisted." So goes Senate Majority Leader Mitch McConnell's censure of Senator Warren on the senate floor, February 7, 2017, as he cut her off and talked over her as she was trying to read from a 1986 Coretta Scott King letter.

> **Get Real**
> Yeah, technically, he invoked a rule to justify silencing her, but trust me, he and others would have found another way to shut her up. That she is a woman makes it a much bigger deal.
> — Suzanne, a collabHERator

In the case of Stormy Daniels, it's a matter of the legality of how one pays for silence or who owns her voice, who owns the narrative. Typically, women and those considered lower on the power continuum are the ones who fall victim to losing in the talk game where voice is the token to play the game and how you use your token is how you win the game. Without a token or with a token perceived as less than, women are either left out of the game or end up being losers in the game.

Is there any good news in all this for women? Will it ever change and get better? We don't know for sure. What we do know though is this: despite women being interrupted, cut off, and silenced, we're still here, and we're not going anywhere.

When You're Talked Over...
Get Over It!
Tips and Strategies

1. Keep right on talking, and don't even acknowledge the interruption.

2. Confidently say, "Bob, I'm talking." Use the offender's name and ditch words and phrases like "please, allow me, I'm sorry, but..." and even ditch the "excuse me."

3. Kill 'em with kindness. "Thank you, Bob, for being an enthusiastic vocal advocate of my ideas." (This is especially effective when delivered with a hint of sarcasm when your ideas have been co-opted.)

4. Create and repeat to yourself an empowerment mantra to maintain self-confidence.

5. Transform the moment through visualization and charge ahead with your voice!

6. Make a big production of packing up your things and then leave the meeting.

7. Make it hard to be talked over by speaking in a strong tone.

8. Let it roll, take a cleansing breath, and jump right back in there strong!

9. Post-meeting, approach offender(s) one on one to talk about it.

10. Post-meeting, approach a leader higher in status than you and the offender to talk about it.

Reflection Questions

1. What is your most vivid memory of being interrupted and talked over?
2. How does the environment or culture support this behavior?
3. What communication styles and differences exist that would allow for this behavior to be regarded as rude?

* * *

Do-Over Challenge

You deserve a do-over. Do you remember that last time (one of many) during the meeting when Bob cut you off several times? And nobody seemed to notice or care but you? Of course, you remember. Not only do you remember, you have perhaps let your frustration toward Bob simmer right below the surface, careful to not let it spill over unprofessionally. You might even be a ticking time bomb.

If you could have an honest conversation in an unrushed, private setting with Bob, the frequent talk-over offender, what would you say to him? What would you want to talk to him about? Take a deep breath, and enter a visualization world that you create, one where things are just and fair—well, sorta kinda.

To ensure your visualization provides a guarantee that you'll be heard without his interruption and that he'll be a captive audience, revel in a bit of poetic justice as you picture him tied to an office chair, ankles bound together, mouth securely gagged.

    Now, what do you want to say to him?
    No time limit.
    No repercussions.
    You have the floor.
    Speak.

*   *   *

Make-Over Challenge

Think of a time when you spoke up for someone else who was being unfairly spoken to or harshly treated. Or maybe it was you speaking up for yourself in your personal life, which you may find relatively easier to do.

How did speaking up make you feel? If you were speaking up for someone else, what difference did it make to the other person? What difference did it make for you?

What prompted your decision to get involved and not be a silent bystander? Where did your courage come from? Did you have to think about it or did your courage naturally come out based on the situation? How can you increase your capacity for speaking up at work in practical ways?

You deserve a make-over. Try speaking up for yourself and others more and more in your personal life as a way to practice. For example, if a salesperson begins to serve somebody else first when you were the next in line, say something. "I was here first." Think about how this could translate to "Bob, I was talking," when you're being interrupted during meetings at work.

Or if the salesperson begins to serve you first when someone else should have been next, step aside and say, "She was before me." Now think about how speaking up for other women at work could short-circuit certain behaviors and reinforce reciprocal ally behaviors. "Hold on a minute, Bob. Karen is talking,"

Chapter 2

OVERtalked

"It took me quite a long time to develop a voice, and now that I have it, I am not going to be silent."
— Madeleine Albright

"My mother was a dominant force in our family. And I always saw her as the leader. And that was great for me as a young woman, because I never saw that women had to be dominated by men."
— Dolores Huerta

"Knowing when to raise your voice and speak is important."
— Alison Morris

As flight #2368 began its descent into Houston, the lead, male flight attendant made an announcement over the intercom.

"The female flight attendant will be coming through the cabin to pick up trash, and the male flight attendant will be on break."

He intended the specificity of gender to the role of each to be funny. Some passengers around me immediately laughed. I and some others did not.

I was curious as to how the female flight attendant would respond to the male flight attendant's comment because I had noticed earlier in the flight they appeared to have a jovial relationship. She had already started going down the aisle with gloves on and a trash bag in hand and was still in the business class cabin when the announcement was made. Upon hearing it, she froze in her tracks, eyes big. No laugh. No smile.

"I. Cannot. Believe. He. Just. Said. That."

When the surrounding passengers heard her remark, the laughter came to an awkward halt.

As a facilitator, I'm also an observer and student of human behavior. But I didn't need an advanced degree to see that a line had been crossed. Keep in mind that contrary to what is the case for passengers, for flight attendants, the plane is their workplace, and the flight itself is their workplace environment. Not sure if that kind of behaviour is overlooked simply because technically we were still at cruising altitude, or if it was the lack of oxygen in the air.

I'm pretty sure if that male flight attendant made a similar comment in a traditional corporate setting at sea level, it would've landed him a front-row, center seat in HR's, "How Not to Get Fired for Being a Complete and Total Ass" seminar. Or at least he'd be assigned to the waiting list!

Power of Voice

Women understand all too clearly that if there is someone in a meeting who will talk the most and talk the loudest, odds are it will be a man. Researchers Chris Karpowitz, Tali Mendelberg, and Lee Shaker from Brigham Young University and Princeton University conducted a 2012 study that showed in mixed gender groups, men dominate the conversation 75 percent of the time, leaving women with 25 percent of the talking.[1] CollabHERators and I feel these findings are inaccurate. It feels to us more like 90 percent and 10 percent. At least!

Beyond that, there is a close relationship between power and voice. The lead flight attendant because of his role, used the power of the intercom system to amplify his voice and expand his reach to the entire flight, a tool likely more readily available to him as the leader. His position was key in using his voice to belittle his female colleague, who, because of her lesser power, limited reach, and proximal inaccessibility to the intercom, was not heard by as many passengers when she responded. In essence, as far as the passengers in row twenty-seven were concerned, the only voice to be heard was that of the lead, male flight attendant. The female flight attendant's voice reached relatively few passengers.

Those of us who lack loudness, who are naturally introverted, or who feel the discomfort of being "the only one" in the room can start to feel like we don't have a shot at

---

[1] Christopher F. Karpowitz, Tali Mendelberg, and Lee Shaker. "Gender Inequality in Deliberative Participation." American Political Science Review. August 2012, pp 1-15. Available on CJO doi:10.1017/S0003055412000329. Published online: http://journals.cambridge.org/abstract_S0003055412000329

our ideas being heard or included. This plays out in male-dominated environments in a variety of ways when gender-bias also exists. For those of us who are confident and extroverted, we can be perceived as having broken the rules and, as a result, can experience subtle and blatant forms of punishment.

> **Get Real**
> I remember once when I was in a team meeting, and the men, nine of them, just kept talking back and forth not getting anywhere. The meeting was supposed to be one hour, but it had already run over. Me and the only other woman on the team just looked at each other knowingly. I remember zoning out and imagining both of us punching them in the throat. It was all I could do to not act on it. I must have been really into it because Pete asked me in front of everybody, "What in the world are you smiling so hard about?" LOL. Thank you for letting me share without judging me.
> — Quinn, collabHERator

Does It Still Ring True?

What do women do when we get our shot to speak? What do we do, when, after enduring being interrupted, we now have the floor?

October 13, 2015, the *Washington Post* published a spoof called "Woman in a Meeting," written by Alexandra Petri. To illustrate the challenges that women face in the workplace, specifically in male-dominated meetings, she borrowed famous, well-known quotes and translated each to how a woman would have to say it to not be perceived as violating "the rules." Here are a few.

Women Overcoming O-Syndrome

"Give me liberty, or give me death."
Woman in a meeting: "Dave, if I could, I could just — I just really feel like if we had liberty it would be terrific, and the alternative would just be awful, you know? That's just how it strikes me. I don't know."

"I have a dream today!"
Woman in a meeting: "I'm sorry, I just had this idea — it's probably crazy, but — look, just as long as we're throwing things out here — I had sort of an idea or vision about maybe the future?"

"Mr. Gorbachev, tear down this wall!"
Woman in a meeting: "I'm sorry, Mikhail, if I could? Didn't mean to cut you off there. Can we agree that this wall maybe isn't quite doing what it should be doing? Just looking at everything everyone's been saying, it seems like we could consider removing it. Possibly. I don't know, what does the room feel?"

"Ask not what your country can do for you. Ask what you can do for your country."
Woman in a meeting: "I'm not an expert, Dave, but I feel like maybe you could accomplish more by maybe shifting your focus from asking things from the government and instead looking at things that we can all do ourselves? Just a thought. Just a thought. Take it for what it's worth."

"I came. I saw. I conquered."
Woman in a meeting: "I don't want to toot my own horn here at all, but I definitely have been to those places and was just honored to be a part of it as our team did such a wonderful job of conquering them."

Be honest. Do we see ourselves in any of these parodies? Even if not us, surely, we have witnessed this from other women. Do we cringe while reading these? I did. I know I've been guilty on occasion of prefacing my comments with an apology (more on this later) or a wishy-washy lead-in so that I wouldn't come across too strong or assertive. I've also automatically deferred to citing the team for credit, even if it was my solo effort, when I deemed it too risky to "toot my own horn." And rather than be ostracized for being contrary, I've sometimes couched my disagreement in very tentative terms.

This was the kind of camouflage that was more likely the case when I was in my twenties and thirties. I'm not saying it never happens now, but it certainly happens now a whole lot less. The human psyche is incredible in terms of what and how much we internalize based on conditioning, messaging, and influencers.

> **Get Real**
> I don't speak up at work because it's not okay for *me* to be the one who challenges or questions. Doing either, one time too many, is enough to get you known as the bitch. I saw it happen to plenty of women who're no longer there.
> — Audrey, a collabHERator

Crossing the Line

"Who do you think you're talking to?!"

When we were kids, it's what my mom demanded from me and my two sisters whenever we got cheeky and "talked back" to her. It served as her warning signal that we had crossed the boundary of respectful communication and that we should select our next words very carefully. Our next words usually involved a sincere apology and show of contrition sprinkled with the appropriate number of "yes, ma'ams."

Disrespectful communication was defined by what we said and also how we said it. Our tone and attitude. It's precisely this distinct flavor of inappropriateness not uncommon in how some men may speak to women. What they say as well as how they say it can reek of an air of undeserved superiority. Choosing our words and tone wisely is a bedrock of communication with others. With our words, we can speak inclusion or exclusion, value or lack of value, honor or dishonor. Because the term mansplaining (i.e., his "schooling" of us based on his presumption that we lack knowledge) entered the lexicon years ago, we also see that words can demean and patronize women specifically.

> **Get Real**
>
> "That's an excellent idea Ms. Smith. Perhaps one of the men here would like to make it." Has never blatantly been said to my face, but having sat on executive committees of major corporations since I was thirty-two years old, this is, and has always been the norm. Is it the tone or pitch of the voice of women that men just don't hear or is it years of tuning out their wives or girlfriends? I don't know, but what I do know is that what I am saying can't be stupid, if it's then repeated by a man who is commended for his good idea or comment. With that being said, I have thrived in my career despite a consistent male environment. Never once on an executive committee have I sat with another woman by my side. So, I have strived to be recognized for my skills and experience, but to be honest, it is hard in my industry to not be seen beyond a gender.
>
> — Cindy, a collabHERator

Theresa M. Robinson

Though I had not heard of the term mansplaining until recently, I've been familiar with the concept for years. My most egregious example would be from five years ago when I encountered John at a speaking engagement in California. At the time, I had been in the facilitating/speaking business for more than twenty years and had been booked to deliver a keynote presentation followed by a workshop. There were to be two keynotes that day. The first to be delivered by another speaker, followed by mine, a break, and then my workshop.

On the break, following the two keynotes, John approached me with a notepad, introduced himself, and proceeded to inform me that the first keynoter had said "um" eighteen times during his talk. He showed me the tick marks he had made on his notepad for tracking purposes.

With his scientifically objective demeanor, he continued. "Do you know how many times I counted you saying 'um?'"

I opened my mouth to respond, but not before he answered his own question with, "Zero."

Again, I started to respond, but he cut me off to provide me with a several-minute-long education on the pitfalls of "um" and some techniques to avoid it. He spoke *at* me and conveyed a belief that I had been merely lucky with my omission of "um" rather than a belief that I had skillfully honed my craft over the past twenty years. I had worked hard on both eliminating filler words when speaking and mastering strategies to ensure they stayed eliminated. Allow me for a moment to mention again what John knew—that speaking is my profession. John's was sales.

Not one single "um." You seem to have this, um, raw talent. I'm here. Let me take you under my wing. You don't have to thank me. Blah, blah, blah.

I tried so hard to not laugh at the irony of his own use of "um" and "uh" as he was educating me.

Mansplaining. Overtalking.

It's a phrase used, in one form or another, verbal and nonverbal, by women to characterize the way men presume the need to explain things to us. Their insistence on "I got this" becomes a means to diminish us.

We got this, sweetheart. Men at work

This might sound too complicated for you. Are you sure you want to hear it?

Let me explain to you what [fill in the blank with what you already know] is.

Overtalking projects dominance and manliness. It's also very demeaning to women when it joins up with mansplaining. The *I've got this* demeanor can become a norm of conditioning, a habit, and can pervade interactions with us. When it becomes obvious to us that men, in fact, haven't *got this,* they will often continue right on in their patronizing arrogance, overconfidence, and presumed superiority.

Get Real

Have you ever been in a situation where you know men don't want to give women anything they believe is too hard? Or they are careful to use certain language to explain things that they think women may have more difficulty with? They think they are making things better for us, but they're not. They're being patronizing and insulting. They don't explicitly say it, but it comes across as "sweetheart, let me explain it to you this way" or "honey, let me help you with that."

— DiDi, a collabHERator

I believe talking over and overtalking go together and are cyclical. First the interrupting happens because men feel like what they have to say is so much more important that it takes precedence over what we have to say. Then because we've been silenced, they miss out on valuable information about us that leads them to continue on as if we're a blank slate, which obligates them to overtalk us (and mansplain) to assert their importance and dominance, all of which justifies them cutting us off in the first place. Let's chalk all that up to faulty man-logic.

> **Get Real**
> If I speak up, people in my office will make little comments. If I say something that isn't in line with what they're saying, or I challenge something they're saying, they'll say, "Oh, are you in a bad mood? Are you upset?" Or they think I have an attitude. I have to explain to them that I just don't agree. But if a man disagrees, his comments will be met with, "Oh, I didn't think of it that way. That's a great idea."
> — Simone, a collabHERator

Simone is one of the few collabHERators who works in an environment with nearly equal representation of women and men. Because she has worked in heavily male-dominated environments in the past, she says that gender bias ironically plays out very similarly in her current job and that the increased number of women unfortunately hasn't made a difference in gender dynamics.

"The meetings are very male dominated. Women in the room nod their heads and speak up rarely, once or twice. They give me the look to let me know they are with me and understand, but they won't say anything. I take it in stride, one case at a time. I give more thought to what I say and how it will add value to the conversation. I don't offer to talk about a problem if I'm not going to offer a solution. I only speak up when I know for a fact that my strategy will be a good solution. That's when I'm confident speaking up."

Though I understand Simone's strategy and how it works for her, I am saddened that Simone's strategy represents what is lost when women don't feel safe and supported to take risks and brainstorm and participate in the spontaneous group sharing of creative ideas that lead to innovation. If we only feel safe to speak up when we feel guaranteed that our ideas will be accepted, that's not a good environment. The point is not that all our ideas be accepted. The point is that our ideas be heard.

Simone keeps her brand of confidence intact by reminding herself that the worst that can happen to her is that her ideas won't be acknowledged, a situation that doesn't signal the end of the world for her. "And if it happens, it doesn't dampen my spirit."

Call it a shield or call it armor, but we wear it a lot. It protects us from being utterly devastated. The one we wear is permeable and multifunctioning. It keeps "the bad" out. *This stuff doesn't dampen my spirit.* It keeps "the bad" in. *I want to scream or kick you in the nuts!*

All Bets Are Off

Though most of our focus is on males in our workplace, other important scenarios to consider are the men we encounter when we conduct business with clients, customers, and external partners that don't work for our organization. Whereas, the ever-present threat of being reported to HR for any impropriety can be a built-in deterrent for certain behaviors, what's to stop jerks at other companies from being the source.

> **Get Real**
> Though many of my colleagues are women, I'm finding differences in how I'm treated by male external partners. It's been a learning experience for me since I started a year ago. I'm working with more men that are not physically located at my office, but I'm having to work closely with them nevertheless. I'm selling to them and I have to figure out how I can make sure that my voice is heard as a salesperson and as a woman because I feel overtalked all the time. They have the mindset where they don't owe me anything because we're not working at the same company. I have to take a step back and look at things as if I were in a personal situation. Would I have said something? I probably would have, but not something I can say in the workplace. I can't lose my cool. In my personal life, I say something when somebody is being inappropriate. Not at work. For example, my team messed up on an order. I was trying to figure out how we could fix the problem and make it right. My external partner is this guy from Arkansas with a thick, loud accent. He re-sent me an earlier email and basically said that "I told you what we wanted, and if you had read it the first time, you would have gotten it right." He used dot dot dot punctuation and all caps. So rude. When I got him on the phone, he was talking down to me and cutting me off. I couldn't get a word out. My focus was on making it right. Finding a solution. It's been a learning experience working with more men as partners and not colleagues at the same company. It's been a testing period for me.
> — Maya, a collabHERator

> **Get Real**
> Sometimes I wear shoes where you can't see my socks. I have these socks that have different stripy colors on them. They're not special socks, but it just so happens that many of the colors are energy center colors. And so, I'll wear the socks if I feel like I really need to make sure that I have my voice on that day. If I need to remind myself to speak up, I'll wear the socks. They also prevent me from socking people!
> — Leah, a collabHERator

Intersection of Gender and Age

CollabHERators aged forty and above possess a certain moxie. Many have reached a point where we simply don't give a damn what people think about us anymore. Yes, we may have our moments and our areas where we do care, but for the most part, we let go of the energy it requires to give a damn. We've come to terms with people judging us, and we've come to terms with the fact that each of us will always have detractors, no matter how unfair or unjust.

CollabHERators below age thirty seem to convey a curious mix of caring with defiant rebellion. This group had the most to say about how younger women may experience gender bias in the workplace when it comes to matters of gender intersecting with age.

> **Get Real**
> We might defer to gender and position. Men discriminate based on gender and perceived age.
> — Regina, a collabHERator

> **Get Real**
>
> I don't let people know my age even if they ask. Even if they're curious as to how old I am, that's something I don't reveal. I don't share that because I feel like I've been bullied before at work. In my past life I had a job where people were ten years older than me and were on the same level. They tried to undermine me and make me feel uncomfortable in my role. After that experience I learned to stop sharing my age. People like to ask, but I just don't share. It's funny because with the older people, I'm not asking them how old they are. I feel like people use age against you. Like that would be a reason why somebody wouldn't get promoted. I don't ever want my age to be a reason for not being promoted. Look at my experience. Don't look at me and tell me I can't have a role because you think I'm too young and then compare me to your daughter.
>
> — Maya, a collabHERator

> **Get Real**
>
> Whenever I'm in those kinds of situations [sexism plus ageism], I do one of three things. Disappear. Hide. Avoid.
> — Peggy, a collabHERator

Same Shit, Different Industry

> **Get Real**
>
> I work in the theater industry which I think is a lot different, because there's such a lack of heterosexual males working in theater. I think that the dynamic is very different because it's not like a corporate environment where the guys in suits are like "don't be a bossy lady," you know. It's people from all walks of life and a lot of people

> that are in nonperformance careers. There are still some of those big-producer-type like personalities where I say to myself that "this guy's talking to me like this because he thinks he's very important, and he has a lot of money and he's the backer of this musical or play," so I have to alter how I would normally react. Fortunately, it's much less for me in my industry than it may be in other industries because I feel like the gay men that I work with love women.
>
> — Ashley, a collabHERator

As aged thirty-something Ashley points out, even in a noncorporate environment, women carry the burden of figuring out how we must change and try to figure out how to maneuver so that we can interact with men. Though she insists that it's a very different dynamic, she goes on to convey the same culture of male dominance as collabHERators working in a corporate environment. Only when collabHERators called her on it, did she sheepishly admit, "I guess that part isn't all that different."

> **Get Real**
> I was an electrical engineer designing test sets that tested out subassemblies of a missile. Imagine something the size of three adjacent bookcases, with a desk surface hanging off the front where technicians would sit and test the subassemblies. When test sets broke, we'd be on call to come and fix them. One evening as I was troubleshooting a broken test set, I heard someone behind me say, "See that. If you break the test set, that cute little engineer comes running." It was Bill, the technician supervisor, who was providing new employee orientation to a new male technician. I also wanted to

> provide a little orientation of my own. I turned around in the chair to look at the supervisor with my pencil poised on my notepad. "Bill, what is your employee ID number please?" They left, and Bill didn't say those types of things anymore. At least not to me. I learned I needed to be prepared for a few different scenarios likely to happen in such an environment. The responses had to be the right combination of funny and "don't mess with me," so that everyone could laugh and pretend the inappropriate comments made were just jokes, but they also needed to leave for the offender an aftertaste of concern that "I hope she doesn't call HR."
>
> — Elizabeth, a collabHERator

The Battle or the War

We've all met people that have knowledge in areas that we don't. We also know people who feel obligated to share that knowledge with us, welcomed or not.

Some men, however, are in a class by themselves. They can possess limited knowledge or lesser knowledge, and yet feel obligated to share it with women they assume know less than they do. Or they can assert their power and put on a display of their dominance while being smugly "assured" of women's quietness and passivity.

If women were to take on and fight every single talk-over that comes our way, well, it would turn into another full-time job. Which of us is signing up to add more to our already full plate?

Certainly, there are some things that are worth our time to deal with, and we would do well to address those issues. But odds are, we are likely NOT going to permanently change a lifetime of habitual behavior with our first effort.

Take heart. Letting some things slide does not mean women are defeated. Men should be forewarned. Perhaps when we are at our quietest, men would do well to tread cautiously. Inwardly, we may be laughing with a snort of derision while fortifying ourselves for other battles.

We got this.

**When You're Overtalked...
Get Over It!
Tips and Strategies**

1. Suggest taking turns in order to rotate who will lead meetings.
2. Have everyone first write down their input and then each person contributes her or his ideas.
3. Volunteer to state your ideas in the beginning to decrease the likelihood of being missed, of time running out, or of having to interject with greater difficulty later on.
4. Suggest to the meeting leader ahead of time to create several formal intervals or checkpoints in the meeting to ensure everyone will be heard.
5. Find one male you trust, explain the situation, and turn him into your ally.
6. Tap into your inner, brave badass and push yourself to talk more and talk back more.
7. Enlist the services of an external and objective group facilitator who can ensure inclusive meetings whereby each voice is heard.
8. Challenge mansplainers with, "You do realize that this is my area of expertise, right?" Also ask probing questions that challenge mansplainers and that indicate your depth of knowledge.
9. Nod. Pretend to give a damn. Repeat.
10. Dismiss or ignore the comments of overtalkers and extricate yourself with finesse and a feigned excuse.

Reflection Questions

1. What distinctions, if any, do you make between mansplaining and being overtalked?
2. Where in your life do you feel your voice is most valued?
3. What was your reaction the first time you recall being overtalked?

*   *   *

Do-Over Challenge

In the learning and development field, facilitators and speakers have a saying, "There are three kinds of presentations: the one you prepare, the one you give, and the one you wish you had given." Likewise, there may be a past situation that stands out in your memory because of how many times you were overtalked or mansplained. Perhaps, though you maintained your composure, you sat there seething. Looking back when you were in a calmer state, you may have come up with several things you could have done or said to circumvent the man-fest.

You deserve a do-over. Write down five things you can say or do at the next opportunity to stop Bob and his band of brothers in their tracks and affirm your presence and value. It may be something you've always wanted to say or do but couldn't figure out how to convey it without prefacing it with, "I know that already, you idiot." Or "Actually, you're wrong, moron. It doesn't work like that. Let *me* explain it to *you*." The greater objectivity that comes with distance can provide you with clarity to brainstorm an arsenal of options to have at the ready to customize on the spot as needed.

1. _____

2. _____

3. _____

4. _____

5. _____

Make-Over Challenge

Your meetings deserve a make-over. Spend some time pondering your ideal meeting attended by female and male team members. Think about the characteristics of the meeting that would make each person feel a part of an inclusive environment. Now think about practical, concrete aspects of such a meeting that point to inclusiveness.

Grab a piece of paper and sketch out an ideal description of the meeting, one that perfectly leverages you as well as others having an equally valued voice. Consider aspects such as room configuration, seating arrangements (i.e., elimination of clique clusters that intentionally or unintentionally contribute to a noninclusive meeting environment), rapport-building icebreaker activity, intervals for dyad discussions, formal agenda with topics, timing, and action items, etc.

Your vision and description should serve as a reference for initiating conversations with team members and leadership regarding transforming what meetings look like, sound like, and feel like.

Chapter 3

OVERlooked

"Your team will eventually figure out what you are capable of, regardless of if you are wearing a skirt or pants, or if you have a low or high voice, or if you have short or long hair."

— Lauren Talbot

"I've learned to hold my ground, be firm on my beliefs, and that you can build quite a following with the confidence that you radiate while doing so."

— Melissa Warren

"I hate being ignored."

— Amanda Palmer

"The competition is over, fellas. I win. *I've* got the biggest penis."

Yes. That's what I said to a group of men in a training class I led several years ago.

If, by chance, you are a man reading this, you're likely reacting with disdain and wondering how in the world I could have ever said such a thing in a professional setting. If you're a woman, you are likely reflecting on and considering your own battles with being seen and taken seriously in a male-dominated environment.

Background.

Twenty-three participants. All people leaders. All men. Not even one woman in the group. All white men. Not even one man of color. Even today, it's not necessarily a position that I relish. Several reasons for this: one is knowing that I may have to prove yet again that my skills and experience qualify me to not only be in the room, but to also lead at the front of the room.

Another lesson from mom: as a black female, I will have to be at least twice as good just to be considered half as good. In black circles, it's referred to as "the black tax." In black female circles, it's known as "the black girl tax"—a double "penalty" for being both black and female.

When the men entered the room, the posturing and the man-spreading commenced almost immediately. Chairs were pulled out from the tables with pomp and circumstance as they sat down, arms spread wide across the table and legs spread wide under the table as if they were riding imaginary Clydesdales. Each man claimed and exceeded his place at the table beyond what one would consider customary personal space.

As I watched and waited a reasonable amount of time for them to settle in and peruse the participant materials, it was clear to me that the men had already discounted and dismissed me.

"Hey Tom," one of them exclaimed loudly for me to hear, as he paged through the workbook, "Looks like I can teach this class."

His comment was met with hearty laughter.

Oh goody. A preview of the mansplaining to come. If one of them even hinted at calling me sweetie, all bets were off.

Get Real

I, too, am a corporate trainer in leadership development. And, who are the leaders? Men. So my strategy begins with having them learn a little about themselves...because that's invariably their favorite subject. When I can logically, systematically, and quantitatively show them why their leadership styles aren't working, they are ready to listen.

— Hillary, a collabHERator

And so, the course began. They overlooked me. They talked over me. They over talked me. The sheer energy it took for me to guide and re-guide the discussion in the right direction proved draining. It didn't take long before they started to engage with each other as if I were invisible. Soon, they began competing to see which of them was the smartest and the funniest. In short, it was an all-out battle for who would emerge as the alpha male of our session.

I was (and am) no stranger to male posturing and male dominance behaviors. I've witnessed it on playgrounds, in classrooms, and in corporate workplaces. And the cost is high— the marginalizing, appropriating, devaluing, and silencing of others.

Theresa M. Robinson

Standing at the front of that room, I experienced so many emotions welling up inside of me. I flashed back to the times when I was the only female or person of color in my classes only to have my presence be ignored as if I weren't even there. I flashed back to the many instances in my professional career when I had contributed my idea only to have it co-opted by Joe Blow Hard. I flashed back to the times when I had dared to express a contrary thought only to be labeled "difficult" or worse. I flashed back to Leroy, Mr. Lawson, Professor McMillan, John, etc. A parade of male offenders.

Flashback after flashback after flashback.

Only about fifteen minutes in, and it felt like an eternity. I chose my words and knew those words would be a huge risk. Of greater weight to me was the indignation of "Today is *not* the day." and "How dare they?!" Pressing me on was my commitment to delivering on the objectives, creating an environment conducive to learning, and being regarded with respect. And on that particular day at that particular time in that particular space, I determined that these men would see me and hear me.

No matter what.

The instant I took a step forward and enunciated the words loudly and clearly for everyone to hear, the group quieted.

"The competition is over, fellas. I win. *I've* got the biggest penis."

I had boldly disrupted and shattered their paradigm. The quiet pierced the room. As they looked at me in shock and amazement, I confidently held their gaze with what I can only describe as *yes, I said it* bravado, mixed with a twinge of *wow, this penis thing is more helpful than I imagined*.

What happened next, I won't forget. From one corner of the room came nervous laughter, followed by more nervous laughter until the entire room was laughing more freely. I had made my point. As a woman, I've discovered that sometimes the "nice and proper civility stuff" in a room full of men doesn't work. It can get me run over.

When the laughter subsided, they quieted once more and looked to me as the lead. I had dared and "won."

When "Nice" Is Career Limiting

When we stay quiet and don't call men on their shit, let's be real clear that we're not being meek or nice or any of those other words used to bully us into acquiescence. Let's put the onus on overblown egos and one-upmanship competition. Though men may not be self-aware or deliberate in overlooking us or shutting us down, make no bones about it, when it happens, it's arrogant and rude. And again, it has a foundation in males affirming their dominance. Not a single collabHERator reports being immune to it.

We all know the age-old conversation that starts like this, "It's not you; it's me." It's a compassionate way to make the person on the other side of the conversation not feel badly or not take personally what we've said. Screw that! To any man who habitually does that king strut, we say, "It's not me, it's you." We get tired of men denigrating us to second-class citizens or to the realm of invisibility. Men's possession of a penis doesn't make them inherently more important, more valuable, more worthy of time or respect. When women are overlooked, valuable viewpoints are lost. We all lose.

> **Get Real**
> We can't just be nice, because then we won't be heard.
> — Sonia, a collabHERator

> **Get Real**
> I can't stand when men keep their legs wide open on a packed train!
> — Ayana, a collabHERator

A lesson in humility may be a good place to start, though such a lesson may be counterintuitive as it flies in the face of the prevailing culture among men—a culture of boasting, showboating, and self-promoting. You see, men likely have had so much practice with these behaviors since boyhood. Consider again Leroy. So much subtext. *I didn't like her anyway. She's crazy. It was never me. It was always her.*

Cultural conditioning has also taught that others' position in society should determine their treatment. If men view women as the relative weaker and less-accomplished sex, then certainly this mindset will manifest in behaviors. Though an admirable trait, humility is not always associated with strength. However, it certainly does convey a strength of confidence that has no need to explicitly announce itself. Leave it to men, and they'll find a way to appropriate humility.

I'm the most humble person you'll meet.

Degrees of Self

Many of us are accustomed to the benefits of growth and progression, especially because they're integral to professional and personal development and are critical to success. Ironically, for some of us, when it comes to our authentic and whole self, due to necessity and sheer survival, we've often felt forced to adopt strategies for minimization of self. When I asked collabHERators if, during their career, they've ever left their real self outside in the parking lot, the responses almost always pointed to issues of voice.

Historically, and even now in some circles, women are perceived as credible when we are silent. When we are audible, we are perceived as noncredible even when it comes to bearing witness to our own experiences. How and what we give voice to are central to our identity. *My voice is me. I am my voice.*

Blair, who is single and the oldest of her siblings, epitomizes the connection between self and voice as she traces her journey from whole self with full voice to minimized self with fractured voice. Though she is strategic in employing the incomplete version of herself, what she shares is further evidence that some women may feel compelled to restrict and architect our lives, our identities, our voices to fit within mindsets and structures deeply rooted in gender paradigms.

Get Real

I used to be the kind of person to never hold back. People knew they were getting *me* 100 percent no matter what. That was before. When I was younger. That's how I was. In college, I would get confused and upset wondering why some people wouldn't accept me just how I am. I might be a little loud, a little boisterous. This is how I am. I mean well. But since I graduated and as I've been working for several years, I'll go in with my 100 percent right off the bat, but I'll scale it back a little bit once I see your reaction. That's how I measure it in the workplace. I'll do *me*, and

> then depending on the reaction, I'll scale it by degrees so that I'm not selling myself out, but it's degrees of *me*. I don't play all my cards. A lot of my livelihood depends on partnerships and relationships, so I have to be careful.
> — Blair, a collabHERator

How many of our voices get self-censored or go silent because we can't disagree without being branded difficult or worse? How many of our voices have initiated a new idea only to be informed that it's "not how the company does things?" How many of us have been told implicitly to conform? How many of us have been called out for not being a good "fit?" Each time a woman experiences any of this, it's an assault on her personhood.

Invisibility

CollabHERator Carmen, in her fifties, and a married mother of three, links being overlooked to being invisible in corporate spaces, which she reappropriated as one of her superpowers. "I used to say that I would make a wonderful spy because I'm so invisible. Initially in the early years of my career, I got angry at being perceived this way, but I finally decided how to use my anonymity to my advantage. Prior though, it's like I was going through stages. I'd be angry, then frustrated, then resigned."

"I'd go to meetings and later get on the elevator where there'd be others who had just come out of their own meetings. They'd be talking about a business situation they probably shouldn't be talking about. Again, it was like I wasn't even there. That happened repeatedly until it became so funny to me. Hidden in plain sight. I remember laughing to myself and thinking that it was never a problem for the people talking because they didn't think I was important enough to be a threat. They saw a Latina at a mostly white company and probably assumed I was an admin. They figured they could say anything they wanted. So, I developed this ability to gather insider information by showing up anywhere—on elevators, in the bathroom, in break rooms on different floors, etc. People would continue to talk because they didn't consider me intimidating or present. I was able to get information that I may not have gotten otherwise had they recognized who I was or what my role was."

During her years of "invisibility," Carmen worked for a big company in a corporate complex that housed many divisions. At the time, Carmen's role was communications director leading a team of eleven managers. Even after she was promoted twice, she continued to be amused at how she was perceived by those within the company who didn't know her.

"I'm not advocating for women to do this nor am I saying that this will work for everyone. But for me, I embraced it because it was preferable to being mad about it. If I were still in my younger days, my attitude would be different. I'd be indignant at the suggestion of being considered an admin. I'd have dressed better or tried harder. I'm more seasoned now and revel in subversion. I still laugh at it."

Get Real

Kizzy is my alter ego. I came up with it after watching *Roots*, reading Jill Nelson, and imagining what modern slavery in Corporate America is like. It's the day-to-day grind of working hard and being overlooked and not seen. It's knowing what you're supposed to do whether you want to do it or not. It's being driven and controlled by a

> "massah" you despise who might reward you with a pat on the head, but who at least doesn't whip you. You get released to go home and come back the next day and do it all over again. The Kizzy thing started out being kind of a joke, but it stuck. I think in many ways, Kizzy symbolizes my ability to compartmentalize. If I keep Kizzy separate, then it's easier for me to say that what she experiences is not me. She is my survival tactic.
>
> — Kathy, a collabHERator

Say My Name

Naming and renaming are associated with power. Who gets to name? Who are the named? Xiaolei, in her mid-thirties and single, relays an incident in a global team meeting where leaders from several regions had come together, some of whom were relatively new to the team and had never met or spoken before. Xiaolei was the only woman in the male-dominated room and also the youngest.

"During the introductions when it was my turn, I gave my name to the group, only to have one of the male participants interject with, 'That's going to be too hard for us to say. We'll call you Shelly.'"

The other men in the room all nodded their heads in agreement.

As if her name were up for a vote!

"I was so shocked that I couldn't even speak. I just sat there for the remainder of the meeting trying to process the fact that my name—and me, by extension—had just been dismissed by the group. They proceeded with the meeting as if nothing out of the ordinary had happened."

"An acceptance of my name is an acceptance of me. When my name is dismissed, it betrays something about you and not me. When there is an attempt to rename me, the implications of that are so far-reaching that you'd need to write another book just to deal with that [laughter]."

"Isn't erasing names and forcing new names on others a big part of how colonizers maintained and controlled the colonized? By wiping out identities and cultures? Such a blatant act of dominance and control. I'm not that stereotypical Asian woman who bows, stays silent, and acquiesces. I refuse to dumb down my name so a bunch of white men can pronounce it."

"Anyway, I got over the shock, and since that day, for every instance of "Shelly" I was called, either during a conference call or in an email, I responded with, 'It's Xiaolei.' I can't remember how many times it took, but they finally caught on."

Unfortunately, what Xiaolei relates is not that uncommon. The issue of gender bias is further exacerbated when closed-minded others automatically behave as though any name that is too difficult to say or is too different from the "norm" is not valuable. I'm not sure if the scenario would have been different if Xiaolei had been a man, but what these men made clear to Xiaolei is that they would call her what they make up in their mind is worth calling her. And in renaming her, they emphasized a power dynamic that in effect placed her at the bottom. Her account illustrates how the intersectionality of gender, age, and culture converge and create interlocking systems of bias and inequity. For Xiaolei, reclaiming her name when others attempted to hijack it, was an act of empowerment that reaffirmed and strengthened both her gender and cultural identity.

What didn't follow though was a much-needed conversation with the "hijackers" regarding why the "hijacking" was inappropriate. According to Xiaolei, "I was willing to put in the repetitive effort to have others say my name. I wasn't willing to take on the responsibility of educating others. I don't want that burden, nor do I have the energy."

> **Get Real**
> I played that name game for a while—changing my name so that other people could be more comfortable. Not anymore. Everybody pronounces Schwarzenegger and Dostoyevsky. I'm half Chinese and was raised both Chinese and American. The name my parents gave me is my identity. I won't apologize for it or hide from it.
> — Zhang Peng, a collabHERator

**When You're Overlooked...
Get Over It!
Tips and Strategies**

1. Disrupt the status quo with an attention-grabbing word or phrase or novel idea.

2. Initiate a private conversation with the offender(s).

3. Enlist the advice and support of leadership.

4. Volunteer for visible assignments when it's appropriate for your circumstances to do so.

5. Seek creative ways to receive credit for your contributions.

6. Publicly and genuinely compliment your colleagues. Giving praise when praise is due elevates your own reputation with others.

7. Ask for feedback.

8. Evaluate your attire and make modifications, if necessary. Consider dressing as if you're the president of the company.

9. Mentor a newcomer to the team.

10. Enlist the services of a career coach.

Reflection Questions

1. When women are overlooked, do you think it happens intentionally or unintentionally? How do you know?
2. What are some things you've done to ensure that you're not unfairly overlooked?
3. What are the short-term and long-term costs of overlooking women?

* * *

Do-Over Challenge

While invisibility may be an awesome superpower when you're a superhero fighting against the forces of evil, invisibility in the workplace is what can kill careers. Being able to distinguish between what contributes to our visibility or invisibility allows us to make choices. In the two columns below, see if you can list those aspects about you that make you visible and those that make you invisible.

For example, one of your ideas adopted by a high-profile client contributed to your visibility. However, your absence from the after-hours reception to celebrate the initiative born from your idea contributed to your invisibility. Yes, some of what you list may seem unfair, and you may not agree with the criteria, but right now, just get them down on paper so that you can see what the perception might be.

Aspects Contributing to Visibility	Aspects Contributing to Invisibility

* * *

Make-Over Challenge

What are the women and men like with whom you work? What do you think of them? What do they think of you? Some of what we and they think may be negative.

And sometimes we can get caught in cycles of negative thinking. Identifying what we want to be known for is one thing, but it's also important to work on changing how we perceive others. I adopted a philosophy years ago that helps with this. Instead of saying to myself, "I don't like him," I took it further with, "I don't like him, so I need to get to know him better." When we can start to think of others as real people and find ways to connect, we'll notice a positive difference in our own energy. And others will notice it, too.

Do you bring positivity to the workplace? Do you look forward to showing up at work? What sensation do you get when you enter your workplace?

Theresa M. Robinson

You deserve a make-over. Write down five positive things you want to be known for by people at work. Now reflect on how you will focus on these things and what concrete actions you will take to make what you've written down be known to others. In other words, it would be bizarre for you to announce to others, "Hello. I'm a person of integrity." Rather, your behavior, actions, etc., will make you known to others as a person of integrity. Portray it. Don't say it. Walk it. Don't talk it

1. _____

2. _____

3. _____

4. _____

5. _____

Chapter 4

OVERjudged

"We teach girls to shrink themselves, to make themselves smaller. We say to girls: 'You can have ambition, but not too much. You should aim to be successful, but not too successful. Otherwise, you will threaten the man.'"
— Chimamanda Ngozi Adichie

"A strong man can handle a strong woman. A weak man will say she has an attitude."
— Pravinee Hurbungs

"Next time you are about to call a little girl 'bossy,' say instead: 'she has executive leadership skills.'"
— Sheryl Sandberg

He directed only one word at me, and I nearly lost it. And it wasn't because I had noticed him staring at me on the crowded airport shuttle as I stood holding onto the overhead handgrip. I have been on too many shuttles in my lifetime to get rattled by someone staring at me. Sometimes there are so many people jammed on the shuttle that you have no choice but to be looking directly into a stranger's eyes—and not in a how-Stella-got-her-groove-back kind of way.

No, the crowd didn't bother me. The staring didn't bother me. It was the word he said that bothered me. The word itself I find absolutely and utterly offensive when spoken to me by a man.

"Smile."

I don't need a grammar class to remind me that when a single word is followed by a period, it's a command. Like "sit" or "stay."

And that's when I unleashed on him.

"Why!? Why should I smile on demand because you think that's what I should be doing!? You don't know me!"

As my voice rose and my eyes flashed with each word, he nervously adjusted his collar and glanced around at the other travelers who were taking notice, but pretending not to. It's amazing how quickly every single person can suddenly have a ton of emails to go through on their smartphone when drama ensues.

Turning back to me, he managed to squeeze out a half-hearted and sarcastic apology. It was obvious that his intention was to only shut me up to not draw any further attention to himself. No real remorse.

"Jeez. Sorry. What's the big deal?"

Technically, he was correct. In the grand scheme of things, it wasn't a big deal. But to me, in that moment, it was a super-sized deal, a deal on steroids, a clueless, careless, thoughtless deal!

I can predict the narrative likely going on inside of his clueless head because I've heard it before shouted at me on the street. *Bitch. You women are so sensitive and make such a big deal out of everything. Must be hormonal or something.* In his mind there was no way he could be the issue. It had to be me. Clearly, I had offended him by minding my own business and thinking my own thoughts while wearing a facial expression of my choosing. If only I had been smiling coyly at him with a sparkle in my eye and a slow-motion breeze tousling my hair. Perhaps then he would have been satisfied and none of this would have ever happened. I brought it all on myself. Just a different rendition of "look at what she was wearing when she was attacked."

Or in this case, what I wasn't wearing. I wasn't wearing a smile.

What shuttle guy considered to be an overreaction on my part goes far beyond what he and other like-minded men are willing to own up to. (I sometimes wonder if it's more a willingness issue or capability issue.) When men expect women to smile and go as far as to insist that we do, it betrays a belief that women are ornaments (i.e., objects) that should adorn their surroundings. I am tired of being informed that I am violating the "smile and look pretty" code. It's just one of many outdated rules and norms of behavior to which women are still held. And if you've read this far, then I know you feel the same way, too.

> **Get Real**
> Women are judged and scrutinized for how we look. We're too sexy or not sexy enough. We're too pretty or not

> pretty enough. We're too fat or not thin enough. One day at work, I overheard two men in our café talking about how overweight this woman was. A man can be bald, fat, and ugly, and it's a nonissue!
>
> — Christie, a collabHERator

Society classifies certain comments or behaviors as microaggressions and microaffronts. These terms themselves can be offensive. Here's why: Attaching "micro" (mis)conveys that these instances are just small infractions and (mis)communicates that they're not a big deal. This is exactly how shuttle guy attempted to minimize the situation. By emphasizing a "what's the big deal?" angle. The term "micro" helps the perpetrators to not feel so badly when they do it. What needs to happen is for women to feel un-victimized and un-harassed.

Often the most damaging offenses are the small, incremental ones that seem "harmless" and "inconsequential" enough when they happen the first time or even a few times. But what if they happen every day? Over time, not addressed, these offenses run rampant and become, in a sense, normalized. The perpetrators remain oblivious to the effects on themselves and on others.

Sometimes it's not a behavior or a comment or a single word; it's a look. It's hard for us to defend ourselves against a look or to prove what's behind the look. Instinct. A knowing. We know when it has that #MeToo flavor, and it's downright creepy. Even those kinds of looks have a stereotypical basis in that women exist for men's satisfaction. That to look at us that way, some men honestly believe they're complimenting us!

> **Get Real**
> Nothing is more uncomfortable than an old-ass man looking at you as if you're a snack.
> — Ayana, a collabHERator

The stories that grace these pages are a testament to what many know to be true—that similar affronts both exist and persist —countless instances for individual women. Imposing gender stereotypes on women, expecting women to take on and assume behaviors that justify and perpetuate the stereotypes, and then punishing or dismissing women for our nonconformity and rejection of the stereotypes—not at all my idea of *micro*!

I've lost count of the random men over the years who've "caught me" looking serious, contemplative, or otherwise. Men that have instructed me to smile for their benefit. How many of these incidents do I and other women have to experience for them to not be termed *micro*? How many *micros* equal *this needs to stop*? Is there a formula I don't know about that qualifies and validates my experiences? These experiences certainly don't feel *micro*. Think cumulative effect. CollabHERators' stories echo the same sentiment. It's the cumulative effect of experiences that impacts us and not necessarily that one, isolated event.

> **Get Real**
> I've got a million stories like this. Pick your poison!
> — Elizabeth, a collabHERator

And what of the reaction women get when we dare call men on it, when we dare to be bold to not comply with and to verbally defy the smile order? It varies. For me, to date, I've been called *bitch, hormonal, mean, ugly.*

> **Get Real**
> When they say "smile" to me, I turn it around on them. "*You* smile."
>
> — Joanne, a collabHERator

After some trial and error over the years, I've devised a strategy that gets my message across to men who insist on saying "smile" to me—strangers or not. Consider the following scenario.

Man to me: "Smile."

Me to man: "How many nonsmiling men have you said that to today?"

Man to me: [blank look]

Me to man: "Zero. That's what I thought. *Buh-bye*."

What I hope happens next is his lightbulb moment. Sometimes it happens. Sometimes it doesn't.

I asked my husband how he would respond if a man whom he didn't know said to him "smile." I had to clarify that I was not interested in how he would respond if he were a woman. I wanted to know how *he*, a man, would respond. He said he would respond in one of four ways depending on how he was feeling at the moment. Either he'd say, "fuck off!" or "who the hell are you?" or he'd walk away, or ignore him.

When I asked my young adult son the same question, his inability to conceive of such a scenario prevented him from entertaining the possibility beyond his quip, "First of all, the only man I would expect to tell me to smile is a photographer."

More telling is what's absent from both these responses. In no scenario (other than professional photography) would either of them respond with a smile.

Yet, that's what men expect women to do. Comply with a smile.

What Men Don't Have to Think About

My husband and son will likely never have to be concerned about responding to another man's demand that they smile. I'm stepping out on a limb here in that I can pretty much guarantee that the same men who instruct women to smile—even women they don't know—these same men would NEVER issue that same directive to a man. Males are not conditioned nor expected to smile and look pretty. And when they don't smile, they are not violating any unspoken "rule" or "code of conduct."

Get Real

When I am thought of as paranoid and overly sensitive by men, my response is that they don't have to think about and consider what I have to. When the elevator door opens in the parking garage and the sun has gone down and there's one man on it, do men have to think twice about whether they should get on the elevator? When men are walking to their car after hours, do they walk fast and grip their keys in a way to be used as a weapon, just in case? When men walk outside to get lunch, do they take the longer route to avoid the construction crew that might make catcalls at them? Do men feel compelled to come up with ways to not be noticed and viewed mostly for their gender at work while wanting to be recognized as an equally valued person? Do men rehearse in their heads how they're going to speak up next time for sure in a meeting? It's exhausting. When I was sharing all this with my husband about these interviews and what we've been talking about, he was shocked. It's not something that

> we're vocal about. We as women know, and we do whatever we have to do. We don't necessarily share everything we experience and prepare for as women. When he wanted to know why he didn't know all this stuff, I didn't really have a good answer for him.
> — Maria, a collabHERator

I don't know if there is a good answer. I think there is a deeper psychology to it all that we miss. Look at the women who came forward and spoke out against Bill Cosby or Harvey Weinstein, for example. Many people were initially judging the women who were violated and victimized, wanting to know why they never said anything before and why they didn't speak up earlier. And then people were judging both women and men who knew what was going on, but who never spoke up. It seems to be easier for people to judge rather than believe or at the minimum to give accusers the benefit of the doubt. I guess it's easier to condemn rather than listen and reserve judgment.

Similar shared experiences, positive and negative, unite people. Many of us within these pages were not shocked or surprised at the revelations brought out by the #MeToo movement. We were more shocked and surprised at the extent and level of the revelations.

> **Get Real**
> It happened on day three of a course I was co-facilitating at a major training organization. At the end of the course, there was a small ceremony to recognize the thirty-two participants. One by one, each was called to the front of the room to be congratulated and receive a gift. Half of the group shook hands with us facilitators while half (both men and women) were feeling so emotional that they gave

a quick hug. At this point we were down to the last participant. Stan, a prominent surgeon, had been seated at a table with two other men. When Stan's name was called, he came up to the front of the room, hugged me, and gave me two quick pats on my butt, while his two male table mates laughed and clapped. In my shock and disbelief, my first reaction was to say, "What the hell?!" As he walked back to the table with a big smile, his two table mates stood to take a bill out of their wallets. Stan then said, "Hey, they bet me!" as if that justified his behavior. Since Stan was the last to receive his gift, the crowd was breaking up to attend the closing lunch on the patio. . . so they didn't see me break down in tears as I walked out of the room. I went immediately to my manager's office and reported the incident. She asked me what else I wanted to do, and I said that I just wanted it documented. I'm not the type to sue. Besides, throwing hush money at me wouldn't hurt him financially. What I wished is that his inappropriate behavior could be publicly posted to humiliate him as much as I was. I wanted his wife, his family to know what an ass he was. Later when I told my husband and daughter what happened to me, they nervously giggled and expressed shock. My husband asked me what I was wearing, and I screamed, "What difference does that make?! You know I wear business attire, but still no man has the right to touch another woman without her consent!" He held me while I cried, but he didn't dare say anything else. Three days later, I was still crying. And when I couldn't hold back my tears, my grown daughter pretty much told me to "get over it!" I thought I raised her differently but it's amazing how much society—both men and women—allow and even accept inappropriate behavior. How can we

> teach men to respect women? My (female) manager sent flowers and called a few days later to ask me how I was doing and if I wanted to follow up. I did nothing more. But I often wonder if I should have.
>
> — T.D., a collabHERator

Many women make daily decisions constantly about whether to speak up or stay silent. We're always having to think about it. To accuse or silently endure. I don't tell my husband, or anyone else for that matter, about every single instance of a look, a word, an action that is an affront to my identity as a black female. If I did, there'd be no time to talk about anything else!

Get Real

When women experience these microaggressions, are we expected to always speak up despite the risk, despite the fact that it's uncomfortable, despite the fact that we might have misperceived the situation? There are no easy answers, because it's complicated. We call them microaggressions or microinequities because the first time it happens, we rationalize it as if it's just this one thing that happens to us. So then that one thing happens over here with this person. And then maybe that one thing happens again over there with somebody else. Now it's different because before we know it, we've got a collection of microaggressions and microinequities. So we start questioning ourselves, "Well I didn't say anything about it the first time it happened, and now it's happened twenty times. Is it me? Is it my fault? Am I doing anything to cause this? I don't know if I can really say anything about it now." We stay quiet trying to rationalize it all and then decide that we need to be more aware and learn how to

> manage ourselves in these situations. I don't know where the speaking up part comes in. At what point do we speak up? The first time? The tenth time? The twentieth time? I don't know. I don't judge any of the women that have come forward with their stories. Unfortunately, the first response from people is "Well, why is she just now saying something now, and it happened ten years ago?" People don't speak up when there's fear, doubt, shame, uncertainty.
>
> — Audrey, a collabHERator

Audrey, a survivor of domestic abuse, raises some insightful points regarding timing. Due to unfavorable statute of limitation laws, it seems like the reckoning deck is structurally stacked against women. There is no statute of limitations on the fear, doubt, shame, and uncertainty that Audrey speaks of that can prevent women from speaking up. Compounded with victim shaming and victim scrutiny, these feelings are exacerbated. Women can feel like they are being violated all over again.

> **Get Real**
> My sister is hilarious. She sent me an image of a woman looking serious and not smiling. And the caption was the woman's response to being questioned about appearing that way with no smile. Her response, "Ya know, people don't realize that I am doing everything I can to have control in order to not kill you. Be glad I'm just looking serious because if I did not have control, I would be punching you right now." We hold stuff in. It's definitely a cumulative effect.
>
> — Dara, a collabHERator

Dara is a single, thirty-something year old. What she mentions about how we internalize "stuff" was brought up many times by collabHERators. Cumulative effect. Some of us carry a somewhat righteous anger underlying our spirit, as if asleep almost. It's like a volcano. It's big, and we know it's there. It can wake up at any moment, stirred by a look, a comment, or act, no matter how small it may seem to others or how out of context. Once the volcano erupts, it can wreak havoc. It's been said that time heals all wounds. Tell that to collabHERators that have buried hurt and anger for years!

Check Your Judgment at the Door

Get Real

After close to a decade of working my tail off, I was promoted to partner. A mere 6 percent of partners were women. It was a dream come true. Actually, I had never dared to dream that dream, so it was more than a dream come true. As we all settled into the New Partner Orientation session in the hotel ballroom, our CEO began to address the eighteen of us (seventeen men and me). After an hour or so I stepped out to go to the bathroom. As I was returning to the ballroom, the next speaker (a senior leader at our firm) was arriving, breathlessly, as if he were late.

Me: "Hi John." (I knew him, but not that well.)

Him: "Oh, hi. What time am I on?"

Me: "Excuse me? Oh, I don't know, I think you're next."

Him: "Well, what time do I start?"

Me: "Not sure. We just received the agenda," I said, puzzled.

I re-entered the ballroom to retake my seat among the rest of the newly minted partners. Only then did it dawn on

> me, John thought I was the meeting planner, not one of his new partners. Gutted.
> — Elizabeth, a collabHERator

As Elizabeth's story illustrates, gender beliefs are pervasive and can impact what we do and say. It never occurred to John that Elizabeth could be one of the partners he would be addressing, so he assigned her a role in his head that conformed to and was compatible with his prescribed gender assumptions. It is doubtful that he ever thought to double-check his faulty judgment against the reality of Elizabeth's actual role—one of eighteen high-ranking leaders in the firm.

Instances like Carmen likely judged as an admin and Elizabeth judged as the meeting planner happen all the time. Has it happened to you? For what role were you misjudged?

It's not just role; it can be anything that has an underlying subtext of male privilege.

After leading a well-received session for a group of fifty oil and gas leaders, I was greeted by one of the male participants who made a point to stop and speak with me before leaving.

"You have great energy. But you don't look like a Theresa."

Ah. The name game. Okay. I'll play along. This oughta be good. Instantly intrigued, I decided to take the bait.

I countered with, "Then what do I look like?" My question was veiled because what I wanted to get at was his mismatch of my identity with his preconceived notions about names and naming.

He took the bait. "Your name should be Tina, like Tina Turner. I love Tina Turner. Great singer. Great dancer. And you're probably good at both. Theresa is a plain, white girl name."

Ah, there it is. Black girls have rhythm. I decided to contradict his paradigm.

"Actually, I can neither sing nor dance well. And your name?" I asked, extending my right hand for a handshake.

If karma has a gender, I'm hoping it's female. Oh, please, please let his name be Dick. Sure, the irony would be wasted on him, but not on me.

"Paul," he replied, grabbing my hand

Shaking his hand, I responded, "I hope you found value in the session, Paul."

Like shuttle guy who likely would never demand a smile from a man, Paul I am sure would likely never have questioned the name of a male presenter. However, he didn't think there was a problem in questioning mine. Why? Because the inappropriate behavior and attitudes of men toward women have been normalized. Our name, our voice, our identity can be co-opted at any time.

> **Get Real**
> I don't know why people are so obsessed with age in the workplace. My coworkers ask, "Can I ask how old you are?" No. Like stop asking me. I'm old enough to fulfill my job responsibilities.
> — Ayana, a collabHERator

> **Get Real**
> I would go to meetings and I just wouldn't even try to talk. It wasn't even worth it. Everything I said would be

> overjudged and overscrutinized. If I said anything they didn't like, I'm over emotional, and if I challenged anybody, I'm overreacting. I was overlooked as somebody who has a voice.
>
> — Trish, a collabHERator

The Clothes We Wear

Morgan, divorced and in her mid-forties, believes that men bring so many traditional notions of femininity into the workplace while women bring in the same ones that they've been trying to subvert. The clashes happen when these forces come together. She offers unique insight using the clothes we all wear. "Metaphorically speaking, men are the jacket and pants of the workplace, which represents expectation and uniformity. They don't have to think about things and whether to conform. They enjoy the ease of normality. Jacket and pants. We all know what we are going to get with them. Jacket and pants. Women are also the jacket and pants, but add to that we are also the skirts and blouses, and the dresses. Because there is so much variety, it opens the door for us to be judged."

Morgan insists that the open door of judgment extends further to include assessments about our hair, our weight, the type of heel on our shoes, our nonhosiery-adorned bare legs. The total judgment can then overshadow what's relevant—our work contributions.

As I am a former Disney cast member, Morgan's comments resonate with me and remind me of the written handbook of appearance rules for men and women, the *Disney Look Book*. In effect during the late 1990's, the rules for professional women in noncostumed roles greatly outnumbered the rules for professional men in noncostumed roles because of such a diversity and variety of appearance choices among women.

Restrictions were placed on fingernail length, nail polish color, nail art, braided hairstyles, hair color, size and color of hair accessories, contact lens color, makeup intensity, shirt sleeve length, strap width of tops, length of Capri pants, earring size, earring maximum per ear, skirt and dress lengths, number of necklaces and bracelets worn, nonpermission of ankle bracelets and toe rings, etc.

The long list of requirements and restrictions for women was at least three times as long as the list for men. An unintended (perhaps) consequence of the numerous appearance restrictions for women is that these published restrictions succeeded in some minds in conflating women's appearance with our skills, qualifications, and experience. Judging women became policy.

In workplaces all over, women can be judged on multiple criteria according to the whim or agenda of the judger. Physical appearance, attire, body type, etc.
The result is language that codifies the judgment. *Not a good fit. Lacks professional presence. Not compatible with company image.*

Get Real

As little girls growing up, being judged—by men and women—is part of our conditioning. We also judge ourselves. It's interesting to watch my three sons, and they constantly do what's a very typical male thing. They one-up each other. "My jump shot is better than your jump shot. I can shoot three-pointers better than you." It's about assessing their performance. Women go to work trying to do something good and, you know, we're

> assessed for the appropriateness of our emotions, our parenting skills, our shoes, our personality.
> — Alexandria, a collabHERator

Dialing It Down

When I was growing up, one of my uncles gave me the nickname boss lady. It's a name by which I was known in my family circle right up until I left for college at age eighteen. Uncle Sporty Boy, as he was known, gave me the name because he considered me bossy. Though I'm the middle child of three girls, he insisted that my personality was that of a first-born son. I was opinionated and strong and also the clear leader of my sisters. I was usually telling them what to do.

My older sister's personality, on the other hand, was more quiet and agreeable. And because she was quiet and agreeable, my opposing traits were much more noticeable by comparison. Only a year older, she was a follower who was content to defer to me in most matters.

My younger sister's personality was similar to mine, but because she was several years younger and idolized me as her role model, she never got the "bossy" label like I did.

Uncle Sporty Boy was clear that he didn't consider me a bully, but that I was the tough, decisive leader to my older sister's soft, tentative follower. It also didn't help that I earned As in school, while she earned Cs. He would sometimes preface his references to me with the cringe-worthy, "And that's the smart, bossy one." There was no acknowledgment that both girls and boys are capable of strength, kindness, toughness, pleasantness, and many more qualities.

To my dismay, the name boss lady stuck, and I learned to develop a love-hate relationship with it even when it evolved into "she's the mean one" as I grew older. On the one hand, I was glad to have a name that reflected a characteristic of my identity, but at the same time I hated that people used it sarcastically to indicate that I was being too strong or too opinionated. In short, not a "nice girl."

Colleagues and clients might be surprised by my childhood nickname and its source. However, the biggest clue has always been there via my primary behavioral style as revealed by DiSC.[2] For those familiar with the assessment, I am an off-the-chart D. My style is strong, but I've taught myself to tame it so as to not intimidate others, especially men, and so as to not shut people down. In my line of work, doing either is very career limiting.

One strategy that I use is my "know when to be big and know when to be small" strategy. What this means is that I'm very strategic about not negating my strength, but toning it down based on the situation. Situational strength, if you will. My presence and personality can be huge and overwhelming for some people and jarring for others who do a double-take on the cognitive dissonance of my big energy housed in a slender frame. I make a point of trying to be deliberately softer, more patient, more empathetic, and more compassionate. My capacity for and high valuation of these attributes are always there, but from others' perspective, my big-ness can overshadow them. So,

---

[2] DiSC is a behavior assessment tool based on the work of psychologist William Moulton Marston. The assessment centers on four behavioral styles—dominance, influence, steadiness, and conscientiousness—and is used in the workplace for team-building and greater self-awareness.

I strike a balance between big and small and sprinkle in humor for good measure.

I also rely on a "pick and choose my battles" strategy. Though I may want to take on more battles, I get very selective regarding issues or matters about which I feel are critical for me to say something or do something. For the battles I don't choose, I file them away in case they crop up again. My silence doesn't mean that I'm agreeing or condoning. It may mean that I'm biding my time.

The Eyes Have It

That brings me to my third strategy with which many collabHERator are also familiar. So are the men who are in relationships with us. Whether we call it "the look" or "side eye," it means the same thing. We may not feel that we can say what we really want to say, and so we let our eyes do the talking.

> **Get Real**
> I use my "the look" superpower at the office, and it works like a charm with the guys on my team. Whenever one of them does or says something stupid or insensitive, I deliver some serious side-eye. They get the message without my having to say a word. It's such the thing now that they even look to me to double-check themselves!
> — Mira, a collabHERator

"The look" is something I like to believe was passed on to me from my mom. If she needed to scold and discipline me when other people were around and didn't want to risk making a scene or embarrassing herself in "polite company," she would deliver "the look." Upon getting her message, I would stop my offense immediately and fall back into acceptable behavior and obedience, having understood every aspect of her message, i.e., what I am doing is wrong and what she will do to me if I don't stop. My mom's mastery of "the look" was so spot-on that at certain times when she delivered it, I would start crying right away.

Today, many collabHERators and I use "the look" in both our professional and personal life. It saves time and prevents us from having to spell out everything. What's so amazing about women is that we can transform our voice, which is oftentimes stifled or silenced by others, into sentiments delivered with our eyes. And what's so unique about "the look" is that women have this uncanny ability to adapt it to the situation and to the recipient so that all parties know that we believe the recipient has done or said something wrong. Though the specific "why" of the offense may not always be clear, the "what" and "who" certainly are.

It's not uncommon that when I lead sessions with boisterous and fun groups, inevitably one of the male participants will go too far and cross the line with an inappropriate remark. I typically immediately stop speaking and give the offender "the look" for a few seconds while tilting my head in his direction. "The look" I use in my facilitation arsenal is not too harsh, and I deliver it with an obvious air of condemnation for his comment and a hint of humor so as to preserve group rapport. I then choose words that match "the look."

"You're married, right?" [Translation: Let me establish if you've been trained].

"Yes." [Translation: I should know better.]

"So, you're familiar with "the look?" [Translation: So your wife has called you on saying stupid shit before?]

"Oh yes, I'm *very* familiar." [Translation: I've said stupid shit *many times* before.]

"So we understand each other, right? [Translation: I won't let you get away with that again in this session.]

"Yes." [Sorry.]

"Okay, then." [Translation: Apology accepted, and I get to have the last word.]

> **Get Real**
> I've always heard that men are scared of me. Not sure if that's good or bad..."
> — Brianna, a collabHERator

Though it's hard to put into words, there are certain nuances in tone that distinguish "the look" for work with "the look" for home. For example, for those of us with children, if we direct "the look" to our small children when they're running around and being unruly, it means, "Sit down and be quiet NOW." If we direct it to our emboldened backseat teenagers through the rearview mirror while we're driving, it means, "Don't let me have to come back there, 'cause I'll pull this car over right now." If we direct it to our partner who says something insensitive, it means, "Back up, and try it again, dumbass." If we direct it to a male colleague who suggests (with obvious gendered expectation) that we take the meeting notes, it means, "Back up, and try it again, dumbass."

Creative variations of these three strategies are shared by collabHERators who've made different adjustments so as not to alienate others who are intimidated by strong women who don't fit the mold.

> **Get Real**
> I never thought the dumb blonde stereotype would have a chance in a professional setting with smart and decent

people. I was a natural blonde until about three years ago. When I was blonde, I kept getting this feeling as if I wasn't being taken seriously in meetings, for assignments, or a promotion. I at first just shrugged it off and attributed it to gender bias, but there were several other women on the team who didn't appear to be having the same issues. One day on a whim, I had my stylist color my hair. As a brunette, I feel I am treated more fairly. And I was finally promoted last year."

— Susan, a collabHERator

Get Real

I didn't have a frame of reference for a specific male role, so when I got my first taste of how we could be treated differently, my reaction was, "What's this about?" I grew up in a household with both parents and four boys where we always could speak our mind. Always. It was never a boy versus girl kind of thing. We were just open and very opinionated. So I carry that. I've obviously had to tailor it as an adult in professional settings and tone it down.

— Simone, a collabHERator

Get Real

We're spending so much time teaching each other strategies for how to operate versus teaching men how to act!

— Kim, a collabHERator

Yes, collabHERators and I realize that we are making adjustments, and that our making these adjustments doesn't seem right or fair and may appear to perpetuate that which we seek to abolish. However, until all things are made right in this world, we consider what we do as strategic tactics allowing us to navigate our environments. We are choosing what tools work for us in the ongoing battle for equity. As is the case with the use of armor and camouflage for self-protection and self-preservation, active battle requires we take on that which will sustain us while we work to dismantle power structures.

> **Get Real**
> I heard messages like, "Don't have big ambitions. Be seen and not heard. Women are the weaker sex." The voices behind those messages began early and were perpetuated by many sources. The voices were discouraging and disconcerting and demoralizing. But one day, one voice spoke inside my head to contradict those other voices. And then another day came, and those other voices were gone. The only voice was my own voice. I'm more than good enough.
> — Trish, a collabHERator

When we don't fit the mold, we can create our own! Our worth is not determined through a male lens. Trish, who lost both her parents when she was young, stresses that we are able to better see ourselves and believe in ourselves when we filter out the noise. Not every message is grounded in what's real. Not every message is worth our time or energy. Among the messages that count are the ones affirming that, yes, we are more than good enough. We've always been more than good enough.

~~Pretty or Smart~~ Smart and Pretty

Hey wait a minute. You're either pretty or smart. You can't be both. You're pretty, so you can't possibly be smart. According to Regina, in her early thirties, these types of comments, stemming from persisting stereotypes regarding a woman's attractiveness, summarize several of her interactions with male clients.

> **Get Real**
> Sometimes my male clients will get flirty. Other times they will challenge my education. One guy was trying to test my education and find out how much I know. He was asking me everything from my undergrad studies to my master's, and about my career and my certifications. At the end of it, he was like, "Well, you're very young, and you're very cute to be doing what you do." It happened to me several times. I just brush it off because I can tell what men's motives are. They are trying to find out how smart I am.
> — Regina, a collabHERator

The smart test that Regina's male clients subject her to probably does a better job of revealing how dumb they are. Specifically, for the man in Regina's example, there is a good chance he doesn't have analogous credentials and was threatened by her. At the same time, he felt emboldened to exude an air of superiority over her via interrogation.

Society has taught men that even if they're less educated and earn less money, they are still the superior gender. *Okay, I may not be as smart or as skilled as you are, but I have a penis. And penis trumps everything. It's my free pass that guarantees me entitlement.*

> **Get Real**
> I am not your sweetheart. I am not your baby girl. And I am not your ma. As today's Time's Up movement continues to mobilize women's voices, I am contributing

my say that, yes, we women have had to endure everyday battles. Let's be real. We live in an era whereby a man can blatantly brag, "I just start kissing them. It's like a magnet. Just kiss. I don't even wait. And when you're a star, they let you do it. You can do anything," and still be elected President of the United States. Like many women in New York, I am verbally harassed on a daily basis. We get honked at by taxi drivers. We get the "psst" by construction workers. And we get inappropriate gestures from your average Joe. After years of this, you'd think that in a resigned sort of way we'd get used to it, but we don't. Though 98 percent of the time I choose to respond in silence, I can't help but feel a sense of discomfort and violation each time I am subjected to whatever the hell affront it might be at the time. I feel I have to live life cautiously and defensively, anticipating assholes at every turn. I wear sunglasses to avoid making eye contact. I wear headphones to help drown out catcalls, but only play my music loud enough to still hear what's going on around me. I take my keys out before getting out of an Uber to decrease time searching for them outside my apartment building. I share my location with a friend or roommate when dating someone for the first time. These are but a few of my realities. So again. To those men out there—you know who you are—I am not your sweetheart. I am not your baby girl. I am not your ma. You will call me by my name or not at all.

— Ayana, a collabHERator

Damned If You Do, Damned If You Don't

We know better than to think that "nice girls" will necessarily be successful in male-dominated environments or competition-driven roles. For example, in some settings being perceived as nice may get us a proverbial blue ribbon for adhering to the prescribed gender code or for being "classically feminine," but when "nice" is perceived as a flaw in competitive sales settings, it can be a career killer.

> **Get Real**
> I have a friend that got fired from her sales job on an all-male team. She was actually told that she was too nice.
> — Terri, a collabHERator

When asked about double standards and whether she thinks that for women in the workplace there are situations where men are harder on us than they are on other men, Terri, a forty-something mother of a son, had an interesting response. "It's harder for women when we make mistakes for everyone to just move on. Women are already super hard on ourselves so now multiply that by others being hard on us, too—especially when we unknowingly invite it. It creates a really bad situation. It's not a good place to be. It's tough. Really tough."

"I'll never forget, early in my career I was working with a group of women, and there was one woman who had a couple of kids and she was kind of a no-nonsense, well-respected woman in the business. She met her commitments with her kids. There were all these other women that were having so many problems balancing their lives."

"So I asked her one day, 'How is what you're doing different? How do you manage to do what you're doing?'"

"Her response surprised me. 'I don't make an issue out of any of it. I don't go and try to explain about how my kids have this thing that I can't miss or that I need to take my kids here or there. I don't do any of that. I do my work, and I do what I need to do elsewhere and not make it an issue. I don't broadcast it. I don't ask for permission. All these other women make a big issue about it, and they apologize for *everything*. Do you see any of these men broadcasting, apologizing, and asking for permission? No.'"

"It was then I realized that, wow, she was right. We women can make stuff so much harder sometimes, and I started to watch that. We invite scrutiny sometimes. And then we try to over apologize. *'I'm so sorry I had to leave the meeting early yesterday to pick up my sick child.'* Men would have otherwise just forgotten about stuff and moved on. It's hard for women to not feel the pressure to prove that we belong and that we can do just as good a job with or without our family obligations. So we hedge, and we apologize because we anticipate that we'll get that kind of scrutiny associated with other's perception of our ability to be wife, mother, and leader."

Get Real

Growing up, it was me and my sister. My dad was a really great dad. He wanted us to be successful. He thought we could do anything that boys could do. We were always very empowered. My mom worked as a teacher, and she's still working. We were brought up with a very strong work ethic and the belief that we could achieve anything. A couple of interesting things: one, we were brought up with this "you-have-to-work-really-really hard" ethic. It was a badge of honor that I took to the extreme, and it just kinda snowballed. And two, my dad was always like, "To be respected, you've got to have a firm handshake like a man." Many years later, I'll never forget going to this lunch with a male colleague after I had been at the

> company for a year. He saw someone he knew that came over to join us, and I was introduced to him. I shook the guy's hand and he said, "Whoa, your handshake is *so* strong!" I was mortified. "Oh, sorry. I thought that's what I'm supposed to do." As we sat down, they were both laughing. I continued, "I thought I needed to have a really firm handshake to be respected." The recipient of my handshake then said, "Well you can, but you have to understand that for some men, that's very intimidating, and for some of our male clients, if you give them a really firm handshake, they're not gonna want to deal with you because they don't want women that are assertive or forceful or what-have-you. That's just not the type of women they want to be around, particularly our older clients." His comment was so troubling. If I have a really firm handshake, some men wouldn't want to *deal* with me—that use of "deal" is so negative. And I was the one that needed to change my handshake. No suggestion that it's men who need to change. This was a significant and memorable turning point for me as a young, professional woman. In order to be accepted and valued, the burden is on me to change versus here's what's wrong with this system.
>
> — Stephanie, a collabHERator

Stephanie relays this is an incident resulting from an upbringing trait passed on to her by her well-meaning father whose intent was to teach her a skill that would put her on equal footing with men, but it backfired when she put it into practice. Many collabHERators are also conscious of the dangers of getting "caught being a man." Certain behaviors and traits that have traditionally been associated with men become further codified within the culture. When women exhibit these traits, some men view it as a fundamental violation of the "natural order."

However, paradoxically, as we know, there are penalties that women pay when we exhibit behaviors that are traditionally associated with the female gender. Terri's friend was nice and got fired from an all-male team. Penalty. Stephanie's assertive and confident handshake got her a stern warning that she would likely alienate male clients. Penalty.

> **Get Real**
>
> A girlfriend of mine in her thirties told me that her boyfriend had made a comment on Facebook or either liked a comment on Facebook about the [January 21, 2017] Women's March in Washington, DC. The post said that all the women who marched were freaks and psychopaths. The first thing I wanted to know was why was she still dating him.
>
> — Kristina, a collabHERator

Bitch Codes

The term bitch is not dead. Not news to you, right? "Bitch" is alive and well, simply repackaged as new words and descriptors. There are many words now being used to characterize women who are violating the "be seen and not heard" gender paradigm. Because men can't get away with the use of such a blatantly sexist and misogynist loaded term, bitch is codified with expressions like aggressive, opinionated, argumentative, combative, difficult, contrary, etc., and women are criticized and rebuked for each of these allegations.

> **Get Real**
> He and the men in his group accused me of being combative. I know full well that if I were a man in this situation I would never be called combative. I speak up in meetings and on conference calls, and I don't allow myself to get spoken over. I speak up for myself, I ask questions, and I contribute my ideas. Those are things that get men recognized and promoted. What did it get me? Labeled combative. To top it off, I was informed in my performance review meeting that I come off a bit too strong.
> — Lisa B., a collabHERator

Being told by men that we're coming across a bit too strong raises way more questions and issues than the feigned feeble attempt to be helpful or constructive. How can we be our authentic self when it clashes with another's view of us? Whose view matters? Whose view comes with a power dynamic attached that will have implications for our career? Can we, without risk, be transparent about how we feel or what we experience?

> **Get Real**
> I'm pretty fortunate. We have a lot of women in leadership. That's not to say that these things don't happen or that they don't exist, but it's a safer environment where people are more comfortable calling things out. If I were in an organization that was predominately male, and it felt a lot more old school, I think it'd be even harder to do that. When women of color call things out we have to be careful. Especially black women. You know that cumulative effect we feel that we

> let build up and then we need a release? That's when we're the stereotypical, angry black woman. We can't win.
> — Gwen, a collabHERator

Quiet, Private, and Unsocial Are Also Bitch Codes

> **Get Real**
> In the workplace, I like to have that line drawn. You don't need to know anything about me that I don't want you to know. It's controlled information. I like to control what you know about me, and I think it comes to the point that I want to stay professional.
> — Maya, a collabHERator

I never attended the Christmas party at any of the companies where I worked. It was a personal preference for which I never shared my reason, though I was asked on several occasions why I chose to not attend. Have you ever felt the pressure of scrutiny when people determine why you're not doing what the crowd is doing and because you're not, then something must be wrong with you? My philosophy is that just like others don't owe me an explanation for their choice to attend, I don't owe others an explanation for my choice to not attend.

The same holds true for any other extracurricular work activities. Each of us has our priorities, and we make decisions based on those priorities. Perhaps some women choose not to participate in certain work-related social functions because we don't want to deal with the same bullshit after 5 p.m. that we deal with during work hours. Some days we get weary. On those days, it's easier to seek a reprieve rather than enter into an extended period of more-of-the-same. As such, our idea of a nice evening does not involve standing next to talk-over Bob or shuttle guy or mansplaining John or renaming Paul while they regale us with clueless comments or incessant boasting.

An Uneasy Peace with Gender Messages

> **Get Real**
> There are still a lot of men in the workplace that don't think well of or respect women, particularly younger women. Men in their fifties and sixties are the worst with their outdated gender notions that they judge us by.
> — Liz, a collabHERator

I've taken on many bumps and bruises along the way trying to figure out the role gender messages play in my marriage. I've had to really think about and focus on what it means to be a woman in my relationship with my husband. Over the course of our twenty-seven-year relationship, I've stumbled through situations that are awkward and tricky for me to navigate. My husband has said to me on more than one occasion to stop trying to be the man. That statement baffles and infuriates me, and so I constantly grapple with it.

Early in our relationship, we used to dance a lot. Neither of us was particularly good at it, but we enjoyed it. Or at least I thought we both did. Then we stopped. I finally thought to ask.

"Why don't we dance anymore?"

"You were always trying to lead."

I didn't even realize I was doing that. I thought to dance was to dance. I don't know the rules of dancing. Did I miss a class somewhere? I never learned the rules. Is the man always supposed to lead? If so, why? Can a woman and man take turns leading? Does the dance come to an end when the man is no longer leading? Can others on the dance floor tell who's leading? If I'm the one leading, does that diminish the other person if we're taking turns?

It doesn't sound like I'm talking about just dancing anymore, does it?

Some of the messages I got growing up, I realize I took to extremes. My mom gave me and my sisters strong messages that she believed were for our own good to make us strong. She would always say that she didn't want us to end up like her.

My mom fell in love with my dad when she was seventeen, got married, never went to college, became pregnant with my older sister, and stayed at home to raise the three of us while my dad worked at a brewery. Newly married and having moved with him to a new city, she depended on my dad for everything. When I was seven, shortly after my Leroy episode, and after a series of short periods of separation, he left her and us permanently for another relationship. A short-lived male influence disappeared from my life.

From that point on, it was the four of us. My mom raised three girls by herself. Because my dad had left no provision for financial support, she mustered up her strength and determination, and she buried her hurt. She took on any jobs available to keep a roof over our heads and food on the table, even if it was just pork 'n beans and air sandwiches. She cleaned houses, she cooked, and she worked the factory line. From the lessons she learned, she passed on to us a fierce and urgent determination to never be dependent on a man emotionally, relationally, or financially. We were to be strong and independent in our own right. We were to guard our heart, our bank account, and our hoo-ha.

> **Get Real**
> We know now the myth that women can have it all just isn't true, not because we're not capable of it, but because even the ones that we love the most like our own mothers, expect so much of us and seem to want to test the limits of our endurance. If I'm focused on a fascinating work project likely to bring me financial reward or career progression, then I'm not being a good mother. If I leave work a little early to get my fifteen-year-old to his extra rugby practice before the final, I get those looks that say, "What's so special about you that you can walk out early?" If I volunteer to help out at the local working bee on a Saturday, then my friends around for dinner that night politely suggest I should get myself a cleaner. And if I tell any of them to take a long walk off a short pier, I'm being rude and aggressive.
> — Jane, a collabHERator

> **Get Real**
> It feels like a choice. Women can either be successful at work or successful at home. Men force our hand to make a choice. I'm very successful at work. I've worked hard. I learned to work the system despite the system. In my marriage, I'm lonely and unhappy. It's like men don't know how to be in a relationship with a strong woman, and even though we can figure out how to be strong at work and still make things work, things are different at home. Men don't know how to be in relationships with equals. They say they want a strong woman, but that's not what they want. Actually, they don't want a strong woman

> at work, and they don't want a strong woman outside of work either.
> — Portia, a collabHERator

Our background experiences shape us, inform us, and then we enter into relationships and enter the workplace, and we're still trying to sort it all out. Mismatched expectations. Assumptions. Clashes. Think about all the space that everybody's baggage takes up when we're carrying it around, then setting it down somewhere, and then picking it up again. We start bumping into each other, crashing into each other.

> **Get Real**
> This whole idea of judging is very problematic. I'm in a situation where I'm not considered a woman because to them, I don't look like a woman, I don't speak like a woman, and I don't act like a woman.
> — Toni, a collabHERator

Judging invalidates us. We haven't been the problem. Judging is the problem, along with a broken system that allows it. No one person can measure up to everybody's varying standards for what is acceptable.

No one likes to be judged. And generally speaking, women play well with others until somebody pisses us off with the sting of judgment.

Our identity and self-worth were never dependent on what others think of us. And because there is never the perfect measuring up, how nice and freeing it is to experience the exhilaration of not giving a damn!

Let's embrace our whole and authentic self!

When You're Overjudged...
Get Over It!
Tips and Strategies

1. Turn the tables.
2. Ask clarifying questions.
3. Provide information that challenges and shatters preconceptions.
4. Invest in caring, supportive relationships, and surround yourself with those who value, respect, and care about you.
5. Invest in knowing who you are.
6. Create a signature self-affirmation[3] and repeat it often to yourself. Let it anchor you.
7. Stay positive and happy in spite of.
8. Get your inner critic in line through positive self-talk.
9. Stay focused on what and who really matters by keeping a gratitude journal.
10. Convert your known haters with kindness.

---

[3] Steps for designing an affirmation for yourself:
- Be clear and specific.
- Believe.
- Say it out loud.
- Say it consistently.
- Memorize it.
- Boldly declare it throughout the day.

Reflection Questions

1. In what areas have you been judged?
2. How does being confident in who you are repel the sting of judgment?
3. What are the dangers of self-condemnation and self-judgment?

*   *   *

Do-Over Challenge
Courtesy of Heather, grandmother of four, and a cancer survivor

    Sometimes we're guilty of extending our judgment of people to our judgment of days. We take those twenty-four hours and sum them up and stick that label on our day. Today was an okay day. Tomorrow is going to be a crappy day. Friday is the best day. Monday is the worst day.

    Your days deserve a do-over. When you pronounce judgment on your days in advance, you'll have that focus for the day and will be more likely to make small choices throughout the day that are in alignment with the day's focus and keep the day on track. For example, "Monday will be kindness day. Saturday will be rest day." Not every day needs to have a different goal. There may be multiple days with the same goal.

    Go ahead. Give it a try for a week. For each day in the chart, pronounce judgment on that day. Then at the end of each day, look back and evaluate if your day lived up to its pronouncement. It's a great way to turn judging into something positive and fun. Share your plan with at least one person at the beginning of the week, and then share with that same person how it went at the end of the week.

Day	Judgment
Sunday	
Monday	
Tuesday	
Wednesday	
Thursday	
Friday	
Saturday	

* * *

Make-Over Challenge

We may have things that we believe about ourselves based on early gender conditioning. We may have been told them, or we may have even internalized a belief as a result of something that happened to us in our childhood. Some of these beliefs might sound something like this:

Girls are the nurturers.
Girls should wear dresses and skirts.
Girls are made of sugar and spice and everything nice.
Girls are delicate and fragile.
Girls are emotional.

These beliefs can get in the way of us being comfortable in our own skin. When these beliefs, consciously and unconsciously, get carried into adulthood, into our relationships, and into our workplace, where they meet up with others' beliefs, they can be the basis of self-doubt and low self-worth. Faulty beliefs and stereotypes impact our emotions, our voice, and our behavior. Sometimes the biggest breakthroughs to happen are our own—we contribute to gender bias when we let it overshadow our individual identity.

You deserve a make-over. You're also unique and deserve to be celebrated. Write down ten things that you like about yourself that defy stereotypical or traditional gender roles and behaviors. Post your list of ten someplace where you can see it regularly. Let it be your reminder to celebrate the individual and unique you!

Theresa M. Robinson

Here's what I like about me:

1. _____

2. _____

3. _____

4. _____

5. _____

6. _____

7. _____

8. _____

9. _____

10. _____

Chapter 5

Passed OVER

"If they don't give you a seat at the table, bring a folding chair."

— Shirley Chisholm

"The only way to convert the people who don't believe in you is to do an amazing job and succeed in spite of them."

— Jules Miller

"Many of the big decisions over progression, promotion, and future career trajectory are taken when people are in their late twenties and thirties, putting women at a huge disadvantage because this is the very time they are most likely to be having a break to have children."

— Cherie Blair

"I'll take Veronica."
"I'll take Eric."
"I'll take Zach.'
"Um, I'll take Marjorie."
"Uh, okay, I guess that leaves me with Theresa."

Does anyone else remember the sting and humiliation of being either the last one picked or one of the last ones picked for teams during P.E. (phys ed, physical education)? Even when you know that you're no good at softball, having it pointed out by being passed over in front of all your peers sucks. And I admit I had zero skills coupled with zero interest in playing softball, basketball, or any other organized team sport. It was a loathing I committed myself to all through school. Only teeth scraping at the dentist was worse.

Fast forward to today. Imagine what women feel like when we are passed over for no other reason than our lack of one qualification—we're not men. The boys club is alive and well, and so embedded that it hides behind rationales like, "she isn't fully qualified," or "we have concerns that she won't be a good fit," or "this is not the right opportunity," or "she hasn't yet built the relationships necessary to navigate the role."

It's Not What You Know; It's Who (with Power) You Know

Being passed over can feel like a door closing or slamming shut in our face. It can leave us feeling hurt and angry at the unfairness. Even if we know in our gut it's a matter of intentional or unintentional gender bias sprinkled with a dose of the boys' club network, what recourse do we have?

Get Real

At a past job, nearly all of the high potentials they identified with low confidence issues were women. So, they pulled them out of the workplace and invested professional development dollars to send them for training to help them. In other words, they sent them to get fixed. But then the women returned back to the exact same environments that fostered their low confidence in the first place. Nothing was done to fix the environment. Women kept their high-potential status, but they remained in career limbo and never moved up. It was ridiculous! The turnover rate for women was so high. I lasted eighteen months.

— Kim, a collabHERator

Get Real

I work in IT, which is male dominated. I've been passed over many times due to my not being a good, cultural fit. Plus, sometimes the men who get the roles have less experience, education, seniority, or track record. More likely though, successful candidates are from the same fraternity or secret society or have a liking for the same sports team or gaming genre. I'm not optimistic anymore about being promoted.

—Erika, a collabHERator

Get Real

It came down to a choice between me and Jeff. They chose Jeff. Chances are he's played golf with them.

— Carol, a collabHERator

Theresa M. Robinson

What You Know Is Not Enough

For many of us, clearly the issue of being passed over isn't due to a lack of skill and know-how. I remain in awe of collabHERators who are amazingly talented, all of whom I consider women of power and tremendous capacity. Definitely, we are forces to be reckoned with. Women of dignity, integrity, and high moral standards. This is a partial portrait of who we are.

Unfortunately, the unfairness of a system that disadvantages women threatens us every day. Here's what others may not see. We might find ourselves battling fears, doubts, and insecurities. We might be questioning if we have what it takes. We occupy spaces where if we fail to take hold and embrace our confidence, it can slip from our grasp at any moment.

Can I do this?
Why am I second-guessing myself?
Of course, I can do this.

Get Real

If being passed over is becoming a part of a pattern, I've got some self-examination to do. If it happens that one time, it may be me and my lack of self-awareness about my qualifications. But if I've ruled that out and have received confirmation from a reliable and trusted source, and then it happens again and again and again—I need to dig deeper. And if I look at people who are being rewarded, promoted, and recognized, and they don't look like me, that's a problem. That's a serious problem.

— Camille, a collabHERator

How His Lack of "Dick-Control" Can Cost Us a Job

It's not whether *we* think we're attractive. What might be more relevant is whether *he* thinks we're attractive. Not long ago in the news, a woman caught much backlash for her stance in not hiring a qualified, attractive nanny for her children because she didn't want her husband to be tempted. Many of us may have judged her harshly, having been on the nanny's side of judgment.

Some collabHERators, however, understood the wife's rationale. As Jeanie, a single, thirty-something year old, put it, "Men have two brains, and you never know when that second brain is going to take over. I think she was being super safe and cautious rather than sorry. It's not like there's a shortage of famous stories about husbands fooling around with the nanny."

> **Get Real**
> A male, platonic friend of mine who is pretty high up in his company made a comment to me that really bothered me. He said that it's really hard for him to hire a woman that he's attracted to. That even if she is the best person for the job, he wouldn't hire her because of that. He said there is a real hesitation due to attraction. Are you kidding me?! I'm thinking, "So you have no control over your dick, no control over your thoughts?!" You know what makes his comment so scary? It came from just one man. Think about how many other similar instances there are of women getting passed over for some stupid shit like that!
> — Maya, a collabHERator

Maya, a twenty-something year old, brings to mind how awful the things we know about can be. But what of the things that women experience that we don't all know about? There can be situations that cause one of us to shut down or go silent or grow bitter. We're not always privy to the cause. All we might see is the consequence. As we discussed earlier, certain things we may hold inside and never talk about or share with anyone. That's yet another reason to not be so quick to judge us or write us off.

> **Get Real**
> I'm saying it now before you ask me any questions. I hate my job. I hate my company. My boss is an asshole. What else do you want to know?
> — Roxanne, a collabHERator

Wholly Passed Over

We all want to feel valued and valuable. When we feel like our gender is a blocker to opportunities or to advancement, that creates an unfriendly and inhospitable environment for women. How do we initiate these kinds of conversations? Whether it's challenging a decision that was already made or getting out in front of it and being proactive and volunteering for an assignment. How do we demand that what's broken be fixed? How can we be transparent, without fear of repercussion, about what we're experiencing and enlist the help and support to work this out?

What happens to us in the workplace when we get passed over can contribute to our isolation. The perception of others might be that there is something wrong with us when we lose out on opportunities. Sometimes we might start doubting ourselves, questioning ourselves.

> **Get Real**
> I don't want to be treated the same as men or treated equal to men. I want to be treated uniquely, based on my personality style and my behavioral characteristics.
> — Anastasia, a collabHERator

> **Get Real**
> You have to choose to be happy. I don't say that lightly, but I do think you have to choose to be on the right side of the scale. That doesn't mean you're not real and authentic, it just means that whatever decision you make, you have to be okay with it. You have to have strategies in place to keep you whole because if I choose to stay in a crappy situation at a crappy company for a crappy boss— and that's the decision I make—then what do I do? Am I going to make everything worse by bringing all my crappiness to work?
> — Taylor, a collabHERator

Being passed over is a touchy area for collabHERators because we recognize that there are valid reasons why women get passed over that have nothing to do with gender. Yet because there are still instances where gender has played a role in keeping us back, it contributes to uncertainty and questioning.

Beth, a human resources professional, underscores the need for men to get more involved. "It makes a difference when a man asks a male colleague decision maker, 'Is it possible that you're not taking her seriously because she's a woman?' There are so many conversations that are taking place whose outcomes effectively deny women access to the inner circle of power. We want men to take risks to speak up and advocate for women just as surely as they would if they were serving their own interests."

As I think about Beth's comments, I'm equating her insights to what we'd do if we saw someone in the act of robbing someone on the street? Would we intervene, would we yell "stop!" or would we call the police? Most of us would do something. What do we do when we know that women are being robbed of recognition, promotion, or compensation? The former is a crime, while the latter is sanctioned activity.

> **Get Real**
> I consider the relationship with my company the same way I consider a relationship with a romantic partner. What if we all stay with our company for the same reason we stay with our partner? And what if we all leave our company for the same reason we would leave a partner? It's about standards. For a partner, we might say we want one who shares the same values. That's me. I knew my husband and I would have to have the same values. There were a lot more things on my list, but values and a height taller than mine were at the top! That's a deliberate mindset about what I want. That's how I evaluate a company. If I am to be in relationship for the long term and not hop around, then that company has to treat me right. It can't pass me over, look me over, or silence me. They have to care. Our connection has to be real just like a relationship with a partner.
> — Megan, a collabHERator

Nevertheless, She Persisted

Leveling for ourselves the playing field, rather than waiting for it to be leveled, means becoming an expert at "the game." How do we get skillful? We can study the system inside out and learn all the players and all the moves. With that knowledge, coupled with persistence, we can "beat" them at their own game.

> **Get Real**
>
> I was looking forward to the discussion with my mentor to talk about my possible upcoming promotion. During the meeting, my mentor informed me he did not see it as the right time to put me up for the promotion. According to him, it was too early. I confirmed with him that I was still viewed as an "A Player," or had something changed? No, nothing had changed. I was prepared. I had diagrammed the entire previously promoted three classes. I had mapped each person and their time to promotion. I had mapped out, at the time of promotion, the size, and scope of the engagement they were leading. I walked him through this, and then overlaid my situation on top of that data. I got promoted. The takeaway for me was that I had to know and understand the system better than anyone else, so that I could make sure to use it to level the playing field.
>
> — Elizabeth, a collabHERator

Here, Elizabeth, provides some pretext to her earlier account of being mistaken for an event planner during the ceremony for new partners at her firm. Notice that her strategy involves a systematic, data-driven, well-laid-out process for being recognized and promoted to partner. She did her homework and collected data to present to her mentor. She knew that as a woman in that environment, she would have to be overly prepared. That she was subsequently misperceived, while attending the formal recognition ceremony for new partners at her firm, made her victory no less sweet!

**When You're Passed Over...
Get Over It!
Tips and Strategies**

1. PUSH: Persist (and Pray, if faith inclined) Until Something Happens.

2. Forge a different path to the same or better destination.

3. Report any slight to a trusted source who can do something about it.

4. Never stop advocating for yourself.

5. Leave with your skills and talent, and start your own company.

6. Write down a step-by-step game plan for each goal.

7. Watch and learn the game. Then play to win.

8. Ask for feedback from a trusted advisor.

9. Seek a male sponsor with a proven track record of advocating for women.

10. Keep detailed records of your accomplishments.

Reflection Questions

1. How can women prove gender bias versus lack of qualifications for roles for which we're passed over?
2. Under what, if any, circumstances should women be given priority in the hiring process?
3. What practical measures can be adopted to level the playing field for women?

* * *

Do-Over Challenge

Think back to a time when you didn't get an assignment or a promotion that you expected. It doesn't matter what the reason was for your being passed over.

You deserve a do-over. Write down a list of everything you had control over that you could have done differently to make you the best choice. Yes, I realize that there may have been unfair forces at work that prevented your move forward. Right now, focus on what makes you the clear choice moving forward. The more you can focus on what you control—enhancing your skills, education, experiences, etc.—the more you will feel empowered to be a bolder self-advocate for future opportunities.

Make-Over Challenge

Whether you've been passed over for a position or an assignment, the passing over act itself does not define you. You are a leader because you impact and influence others around you, both consciously and unconsciously. The important question is do you consider yourself a leader? Why or why not?

You deserve a make-over. Your leadership is not contingent upon your position or title or lack thereof. Own your leadership narrative. A change in perspective and a change in mindset are powerful enough to activate your inner leader.

Think about the current state of your character and the traits you possess. Write down ten leadership qualities that you possess. Afterwards, reflect on your list and consider what actions and behaviors support each trait.

My leadership traits:

1. _____

2. _____

3. _____

4. _____

5. _____

6. _____

7. _____

8. _____

9. _____

10. _____

PART II

What We Do to Ourselves

"Self-sabotage is an unconscious subversion, disruption, or obstruction to hinder your own cause or endeavor. You consciously have a desired outcome, but you work against yourself unconsciously."

— Evelyn Lim

Chapter 6

OVERachieve

"Done is better than perfect."
— Sheryl Sandberg

"I can be a bit of an overachiever and always dance that line of balance between giving myself to work versus giving time to myself and loved ones."
— Kathryn Budig

"If you flatter me, or if you look at me the right way, I will kill myself to please you. It's very painful to be an overachiever."
— Louise Bourgeois

As a kid, I had a deep-seated fear that took me years to outgrow. My fear was cyclical and reared its ugly head in my life daily, sometimes with the help of my sisters. All it took for my fear to be triggered were their well-timed taunts.

"The Boogey Man's gonna getcha tonight!"

"There's a monster under your bed!"

"That monster in the closet's gonna getcha!"

My kryptonite was my irrational fear of the dark. My fear could reduce me to a quivering and cowering mess. I always slept with my bed covers over my head, so I couldn't see the dark outside. I convinced myself that if I couldn't see the dark, then that means the dark isn't there. The covers were my barrier, my shield, my protection.

My sisters used my fear against me. It was as if seeing my strength of personality evaporate at sundown caused their strength to increase. They would wait until nearly our bedtime and then proceed to tease me relentlessly about the Boogey Man, who all kids know comes out only at night. I barely slept a whole night through. When the *Poltergeist* movie came out, I was convinced my sisters had something to do with it!

The Biggest Boogey Man of All

When we were children, fear was sometimes the unfortunate by-product of our boundless creativity and imagination. Fear found a place in our thoughts and threatened us at times when we felt most vulnerable and alone (i.e., alone at night in the dark). Our childhood fears always involved "what might be lurking out there."

That was then. With adult fears, it's more a matter of "what might be lurking inside ourselves" that we are unable or unwilling to confront.

Some of us have mastered our fears, which is different from overcoming them. And many fears tend to be internal rather than external.

> **Get Real**
> I hide behind work and make multiple excuses that I am doing enough to excuse myself for still not addressing certain things. Work still does define me. There is not much outside that bracket, and I kind of like it in an unkind-to-me sort of way.
> — Cindy, a collabHERator

In other words, there may exist a fear of dealing with issues surrounding self. Overachieving at work provides the perfect "cover" like the one I put over my head as a kid to shield me from the dark. When we are so busy overachieving, it creates the perfect excuse and distraction to not have to deal with ourselves. What's really behind some women going into overdrive to achieve at work to the detriment of ourselves, our health, our happiness, and our relationships? And what is the cost if we're overachieving at a soul-destroying job?

> **Get Real**
> And, for the record, I don't claim to be too "busy" any more. It doesn't feel authentically spiritual to me. I bet you know what I mean.
> — Vanessa, a collabHERator

High Achiever Versus Overachiever

> **Get Real**
> High achievers shoot for the best. Overachievers shoot themselves for the best.
> — Terry, a collabHERator

"I don't have time to be sick" or "I can't afford to be sick" (and not in the monetary way). Admit it. You've said this to yourself before, haven't you? I have. I remember once working on a training proposal with a very tight deadline. Not having completed the work yet, I woke up on the morning it was due with a sore throat and stiff joints, and one of the first thoughts that hit me was, "Oh no, I can't be sick. This proposal is due before five." Sickness doesn't consult our schedule. Shoveling Zicam and vitamin C down my throat was more of an effort to save the work versus trying to stave off the flu.

And what about that "oh no" feeling when our child gets sick at the most inopportune time (as if getting sick could happen at an *opportune* time!). It's a very panicky feeling waking up and discovering our child is too sick for pre-school and we're scheduled to deliver a high-stakes presentation to a key client. What makes it panicky is that we also have no backup. Our partner is out of town on a business trip. No relatives or friends close by.

Brenda, in her mid-fifties and mother of two university-aged children and a caregiver to a mother with Alzheimer's, thinks back to when her kids were younger. A part of what is termed the "sandwich" generation in that she is parenting children while caring for an aging parent(s), Brenda highlights the lengths we are willing to go to in order to preserve the work. No matter what, the work must go on!

> **Get Real**
> I remember so clearly dropping off my sick child at daycare, just so I could race to the office, finish a few important assignments, and gather my stuff to work at home for a few days, knowing full well I'd be called within a couple of hours to come pick her up. Not just once, but multiple times. What we do to ourselves!
> — Brenda, a collabHERator

In addition to us knowing that people at work may already be judging our ability as working mothers to handle the demands of work, there is nothing quite like that feeling we get when we realize there's no alternative except calling in to work with the news that we can't come in—and providing the reason. Sick child. No back-up childcare.

It's like working so hard against all odds to win at something and then having to concede defeat. And even though our boss might say, "I understand. These things happen. Take care of your child. We've got it covered," what we hear is, "You can't handle both. You should be home caring for your child. I'll have Larry give the presentation. He's here today, and he doesn't have sick child issues."

> **Get Real**
> Overachievers, I think, place expectations on themselves that others don't. My husband has reminded me several times that I'm doing stuff that nobody else is doing and then getting stressed out about it because I'm not achieving it. He said to me, "Nobody else is measuring their success that way."
> — Staci, a collabHERator

Being an overachiever oftentimes means that anxiety becomes our normal state. We're pumped so full of adrenaline and cortisol (stress hormones) that our body, mind, and spirit become addicted to the drama. You know that girlfriend who we insist lives for the drama? Well, guess what? She's us! We are the girlfriend who's addicted to the drama of overachieving. Just because we've managed to limit the drama to more "worthy" pursuits and goals makes it no less of an issue. The self-imposed pressure to overachieve and the resulting addiction keeps us stuck rather than allowing us to address what's really going on and then create what we need and want. Paradoxically, by overachieving we sabotage ourselves as women while trying to excel in a system pitted against us.

And when we're stuck, we don't even know how ridiculous we start sounding. We don't realize that it's not anybody else's responsibility to take care of us. We think we have to seek permission and then wait for it in order to get help and support.

> **Get Real**
> I've just been drowning in work lately. Just trying to keep my head above water and failing. Some of my colleagues suggested that I should get an executive coach. I believe discussions have started, but I'm not sure approval has been granted yet for me to even have a coach.
> — Sofia, a collabHERator

Be Clear on the Cost

Salome and Cindy, both in their forties and highly successful in their careers, don't know each other. However, their stories tie them together in illustrating the potential of work to consume and devastate us when we pursue it as the means of life success. Not all women are mothers, and not all women aspire to motherhood, yet notice through them both how our pursuits at work can spill over and impact the most personal of our desires and choices and can wreak havoc in ways we've never imagined.

> **Get Real**
>
> Imagine receiving the worse news a woman could ever receive, "You will not be able to have children." I admit I was only momentarily devastated because deep down inside, I really never wanted to have children. I took pride in being an extremely busy, overachieving, workaholic, educated professional. I often felt sorry for my girlfriends who seemed so burdened with their children. Family and friends would often ask my husband and I about having children. I never gave a real reason or avoided the question. Work was my priority. I remember one crazy night, I stayed in the office until 4 a.m., went home, took a nap, and returned to the office by 8:30 a.m. The hard work paid off, at least so I thought. I quickly began to climb the corporate ladder, rung by rung. From analyst to assistant director to corporate director. During the climb, my health suffered. I gained a tremendous amount of weight and suffered with reproductive issues. Suffer. That's exactly what I did. I suffered and ignored it. Chris, my physician and also my friend, was always reminding me to come in for a visit, but I was always too busy. Then one day the pain became so intense, I could no longer ignore it. Uterine cancer. My world stopped. After months of surgeries, recovery, and self-reflection, I realized that cancer saved my life and woke me up to the reality that I must love myself more than I love my work.
>
> — Salome, a collabHERator

> **Get Real**
>
> I made a conscious decision when I was in my early twenties that I wanted to be successful. I am from a generation who when we were young thought we could have it all, a wonderful career, a wonderful marriage, and wonderful children. But I got divorced at thirty, just as my career really began to take off. And no children. I lost sight of two out of three of these things because I was determined to succeed. I ran at pace up the ladder, working ridiculous hours to constantly compete with my male counterparts. Then at forty-five, I stopped and questioned myself. Who am I trying to prove anything to? And for what purpose? Money? Status? I genuinely didn't know the answer. I am very proud of my achievements, and I know my strengths. But I'm still not convinced no matter how hard I work that much has changed for women no matter how credible I might be. I still have to strive to be an equal both in regard to remuneration and effort put in. I may not have it all, but I will not give up trying to make positive changes, not just for women, but for every aspect of diversity. I am not convinced I will see a true balance in the working world in my lifetime, but in the wise words of Bob Dylan, "The times, they are a-changin."
>
> — Cindy, a collabHERator

If Your Biggest Relationship Is with Work

When I sat down with Jade, a married mother of two in her forties, the first thing I noticed was her glow. It blew me away! She was radiating from both the inside and outside. Coming from Jade, this was a most surprising and curious development especially because when I first met her years ago, she couldn't have been more different. Before we started talking about the book project, I had to find out the source of her radically different appearance.

"When I look at you, Jade, I notice that everything about you is different—your hair, your face, your smile, your essence. Everything. You're so different. You look ten times happier than when I first met you in Phoenix. There was something about you in Phoenix that was so—how do I say this—so sad, dark, empty, deflated. Today, you radiate a certain light, a certain glow, and it's more than hair and makeup!"

Smiling even more, Jade opened up. "I've been on this journey since we first met. Right now, I'm in a place where I'm more relaxed for sure. I started to learn there are things that I do to myself that lead to me feeling overdone in a lot of areas. And I've started to forgive myself. Initially, I thought I shouldn't even say that to myself because I didn't know that I need forgiveness. But I realized that I was holding myself to such a high standard that was sometimes too hard to meet. I was always in this cycle of 'I'm not enough' or 'I'm not doing this' or 'I'm not doing that.' I was focusing on the things I'm not rather than focusing on the things I am. So, my outlook now is different."

Jade continued, "I was telling somebody at work yesterday who was complaining about stress that I'm not going to allow work to stress me out to the point where it's impacting my health and my well-being, because I've been there. I've been at the point where because of the demands at work, combined with the demands of home, along with my own expectations of myself, it put me on the edge every day of trying to get through the day and not being able to appreciate the wonderful things that I have or enjoy the moment. Maybe it's the maturing process."

Jade has discovered the secret of what makes her smile on the inside. No easy feat for overworked, overstressed, overachieving working women! Her narrative illustrates what happens when experiences grow up and becomes wisdom, when insight gives you different "I-sight." Even when recounting painful experiences, Jade maintained her internal smile for our entire conversation.

I remember reading somewhere that on average, working professionals don't crack our first smile on Monday until after 11 a.m. Could it be that Monday is the most dreaded day of the week because for some, it means a new cycle of work, work, work is beginning. For others, who don't stop working even during down time from work, Monday means it's time to ramp up what we've already been doing. When we get to the root of what it is that we're really dreading, we might even realize that we control the dial concerning stress more than we think.

> **Get Real**
> My superpower is also my kryptonite.
> — Ana, a collabHERator

Striving for Perfection and Approval

Fifty-something-year-old Lisa, a communications executive and mother of a son, has a very interesting take on what she calls having an overachiever gene that gets activated during childhood. "When I think about the difference between boys and girls in school, especially when some people insist that boys are more relaxed, I think about my son back when he was at a very young age and his childhood friend, Amanda. If the teacher gave Amanda anything less than a hundred percent on her work, she would cry and take it personally."

"In my mind, she was probably the kind of child who is going to kill herself, at least figuratively if not literally. I think about myself at that age being an overachiever, and I realize that there is something in females especially that drives us. Society has reinforced that. Girls are made to feel that we have to be perfect, whereas boys only need be brave."

"Overachieving is even more problematic for women of color. As a daughter of black, working-class parents, one of the things I heard is that I must be twice as good as anybody else to be considered half as good. You're nodding your head because you know this already. That was instilled in us from an early age. That's in addition to what white women face. So, add on to that and it's four times as good. You know. The 'black girl tax.'"

Relying on Work for Identity and Self-Worth

Our position does not determine who we are. Who we are is way more important than what we do or what possessions we have.

> **Get Real**
> I want to be a caregiver. It's a deep need of mine. I'm also a high achiever. I want to achieve. Some women might say that it's not possible to be both and have it all, and I'm like yes, it is. It's totally possible. The problem is that there's so much feeding the need to be perfect in what we do. Trying to be a perfect caregiver and a perfect achiever—it's very difficult to break that cycle within ourselves. I think there's a huge amount that we personally do to ourselves. We think that we have to achieve that next thing, snag that next role, be at the top of everything, be the best this or the best that. It's like we're constantly

> looking for ways to validate our worth. For me that was a big issue, looking for reasons for people to love me and wondering if people would still love me if I didn't have this title or this great paycheck. That's how deep it went for me. I was always questioning am I worthy enough: worthy of happiness, worthy of an extra half-hour to read, worthy of saying "no, I'm not going to do that."
>
> — Michele, a collabHERator

Overachieving to Numb the Pain

The busier we are, the less time we have to be with ourselves and think. *If I can work myself out of feeling anything, then there's no problem.* It's like going so long without food that you reach a point that you feel no longer hungry. No, we didn't just beat the system. What this means is that we have worked ourselves into such a state of overachiever normalcy that we lose the awareness to know that we're in danger. Overachieving gets physiologically normalized.

> **Get Real**
> I've lived my life in "O" mode not only as an adult, but also as a child. The reality of it for me was shaped by three events that happened before I was eighteen. Raped at age three. Molested at age twelve. Gripped by seizures from age three to twelve. Those experiences taught me at an early age that there was power in having control of my life, my body, my environment, and my emotions. I vowed never to let another person take advantage of me or control my fate in any way. I became hypersensitive to my surroundings and people, and I developed an extreme focus on achievement and being in control in every aspect

> of my life. I was friendly but kept my guard up and overanalyzed every word and action in my relationships. Academically, I learned how I learned so that I could make the best grades, and that meant not only taking notes, using flash cards, but also tutoring others so that I could hear myself say the words out loud. For me, overachieving, overanalyzing, and overdoing were about survival, and I found value in that.
> — Monique, a collabHERator

Why Seeking Relief through Food, Wine, and Chocolate Doesn't Work

When we're feeling over it, sometimes we seek solace in the external, which gives us immediate, temporary gratification followed usually by regret. Dietitian Dr. Jo Lichten explains why. "When we reach for a drink or something sweet or salty because we're feeling blue, stressed, or overworked, we can blame it on the addictive qualities of these items which primes our brain with 'feel good' chemistry. But that's not going to get us anywhere in terms of relief. Yes, there's research that demonstrates that alcohol and certain foods do offer a temporary uplift in our mood and a reduction in our stress level. But, as we all know, that good feeling is just fleeting. The long-term result is actually more stress."

> **Get Real**
> I know I drink too much, but it's kind of how I make it through. It's not how life's supposed to be.
> — Mia, a collabHERator

Dr. Jo continues, "We can get relief while preventing these binges in several ways. One way is to examine our need for perfectionistic, dualistic thinking. As long as we strive for the unrealistic model of perfection (in which we are either good or bad, either a success or failure), we will continue to feel inferior, inadequate, and undeserving. And, it is this feeling that leads to our need to binge."

In talking with collabHERators, I wonder how often we reach for these items primarily because we want to escape or numb ourselves to whatever is going on internally or whatever is happening externally. Dr. Jo insists that we have to treat ourselves right. "We have these cravings for certain foods and alcohol when we aren't getting what *we* need. Listen to your body. Listen to your heart. So often we hear the golden rule to 'treat others like we want to be treated.' Let's treat ourselves like we want others to treat us. Let's stop waiting for others to give us the respect and treatment we deserve. Let's give that gift to ourselves. Let's remind ourselves that each of us is a whole person. If we fail in one area, that's just a small part of who we are. For example, don't get too caught up with weight. Again, that's one aspect. It's not all of who we are."

Get Real

I'm starting to appreciate me more and be more okay with my imperfection. Even still, I really want to lose some weight right now. We've all been there many times, but I decided I'm not normally like this. Even that realization is a process. I haven't lost the weight and it makes me frustrated, but you know, it's a goal I'm going to do my best on. That's the mindset I want to put into practice. It's okay if I don't get that workout in today or if I don't eat exactly the way I want. I'm okay because there's always

> tomorrow. There was a time when that wouldn't have been the case. I would've been obsessed with figuring out how to make everything work. I would have been consumed with looking at my clothes and insisting that I'm going to fit into them. That's so frustrating every day. I decided, instead, to just buy myself some bigger clothes—not a whole wardrobe because I don't want to be here forever. But I need to feel good going to work or wherever I need to go. This won't be my size forever, and so I'm not going to worry about it. That seems like a small thing, but it's helping me see how I'm changing and becoming more relaxed and okay with myself.
> — Courtney, a collabHERator

Hope and Healing for Perfection

If you're an overachiever, you're very familiar with the perfection gene. Overachievers share this gene, but it (wo)manifests itself in a myriad of ways and often leads to unhappiness, exhaustion, burnout, and health issues.

> **Get Real**
> None of this is easy. The first and most difficult step is to be honest with ourselves. We need to work through, probably with the help of a professional, what is normal and what is not. When we've been submerged in a sea of abuse, some of it so subtle that we don't realize, it's not okay. Our perspective can be skewed. The second step is to have the courage to do something to change it. When we stand up to people who have been the perpetrators of abuse, even the ones we've loved the most, we'll cop some criticism, and we'll need our courage to back ourselves. It took me two years to find my inner goddess, and she

hasn't let me down yet. The courage that it took to send my fourteen-year-old to military boot camp for ten days was almost overwhelming, but the respectful young man who now lives with me proves that my own wisdom and intuition were the truth that I needed to follow.

— Jane, a collabHERator

Get Real

For my generation, the boomers, there were less options then. We worked our tails off, and we did it earlier in our career more than later. That's what you did. You didn't have a choice. Well, okay, everyone has a choice. But you kept your head down, and you worked with your head down. Now we've got this whole generation of millennials coming in and they're saying, "Whoa, this sucks. This is nuts." Why can't we be happy for that sentiment that we've wanted to say all along? But it's coming from them. Why can't we be happy for that? How can we be productive or capable of our full potential when we're exhausted, burned out, and unhappy? There's so much that I think we can learn from millennials, and I truly believe we are living in an interesting time because within the current movements there is also unique stirrings amongst gen Xers and boomers who are saying, "You know what, those millennials are on to something. I'm not doing this, and I'm not waiting for change. I can go and create change for myself." I'm not saying it's easy.

— Beverly, a collabHERator

Get Real

God was gentle with me at first, whispering to me to slow down. Then when I received a life threatening diagnosis, I figured that God had resorted to telling me what I needed in a way I would understand. "Sit your ass down!" From that experience, I started to contemplate slowing down and why I don't seem to know how to do it for myself.

— Gabriella, a collabHERator

Get Real

Work was very stressful. More than the normal stress of work. Our business wasn't performing so there was just a lot of stress in general. We had gone through a couple of restructurings, and I was right in the center of it. It was a lot of work. Hard work. It's not fun work. So I'm working really long hours to the point of getting up early. Whereas I used to get up early and work out and then go to work, I was getting up early and working and then going to work. The cycle was take my kids to school, go to work, work, come home and have dinner with my family, work, get little sleep, wake up, work. It went on like that long term. It got to the point where it started to affect my health. At the time I didn't know that stress was the cause of the health issues, but I started having these mysterious and chronic health issues.

— Jade, a collabHERator

Jade, who earlier shared her new outlook, and a few collabHERators were "forced" into a sabbatical when health and well-being issues could no longer be overlooked. Whereas, Jade was able to negotiate with her company for a mutually agreed-upon sabbatical not mandated by a doctor or mental health professional, others were not so fortunate. Laurie, single and in her forties, was forced to take a leave, during which time she was terminated. Evie, a divorced, single mother, was made to jump through hoops to provide documentation that an extended leave was medically necessary. Once she secured the required paperwork, she took advantage of the entire leave period and used the latter portion of it to secure another position because she knew there was no way she was returning to her old one.

Nervous breakdown, cancer, brain fog, chronic pain, exhaustion, hypertension, migraines, shingles, burnout, hives, fatigue, mystery illnesses. No matter the specificity, or lack thereof, of the diagnosis, the root cause of what ails us can often be traced to enormously high and unmanaged, chronic stress levels. The stories about health-related crises that force us to slow down and stop to rest contain many striking similarities. The way some of us overwork ourselves is killing us! We live in a society where taking rest is an act of courage. For some, who have to fight for it, it's an act of rebellion.

How can we leverage those times when we do feel the courage to do something to better our situation? We all get what I call these glimmers of courage to know what's right for us and what's not. Because the glimmer is fleeting, we can quickly lose it and subsequently succumb to the demands. Think of these glimmers as impulses, normally what we associate with the negative. When is acting on impulse a good thing? When it allows us to save ourselves!

Several collabHERators commented on making a critical decision to benefit their well-being and then having to act on it quickly before an opportunity arose to provide an excuse for changing their mind. Whether it's a decision to quit a job before securing another one or it's-a-done-deal decision to take a sabbatical made during a weekend, too much thought and deliberation can doom our prioritization of self.

> **Get Real**
> I didn't want to overthink it and talk myself out of it [request for a sabbatical].
> — Evie, a collabHERator

We become paralyzed with doubt and fear and the brain goes into overdrive to de-escalate the crisis.

I guess I can make it to Friday.

Things will let up soon. I just have to hang in there a little while longer.

It's not so bad.

They'll think I can't work under pressure.

I just need to focus.

I can make it through this.

This isn't a good time for me to be tapping out.

It's easier for us to legitimize and rationalize than it is for us to feel the truth of what's happening to our well-being.

> **Get Real**
> Several doctors wanted to prescribe me antidepressants. I'm not what you'd call an anti-medication person, and I believe it can be good if it's the right thing, but I wanted to try some other things first before going that route. And it seems doctors want to go that route. I didn't know much about depression. I've heard people talk about it though. As I started to learn more, one of my doctors gave me a brief assessment and said that I might have mild depression. She wanted to give me something to take. And again, I didn't want to do that just yet. There just had to be some other things I could do. Her response was that

> she has so many patients who take something every day and that it's nothing for me to worry about.
> — Jade, a collabHERator

So, You Want to Take a Sabbatical?

Some of us may decide we need a time-out from work for a length of time such that a simple vacation just won't do. Sure, two to four weeks off is better than nothing. But what about those of us who know our well-being status has reached a critical stage? For women who want the courage to ask for a sabbatical, I asked Jade to provide insight on how she was able to negotiate a year-long sabbatical from her job and then return without any detriment to her career mobility.

"First thing, my husband and I had a conversation to ensure we were both on the same page about this being something we were going to pursue. When I went in to have the conversation with my leadership, I positioned it as a win-win. I was prepared. If leadership had come back with 'A,' I was coming back with 'B.' If they had then said 'C,' I'd have come back with 'D.'"

"I put a lot of preparation into how the dialogue could go. It never got to the point where it was ever a 'no' from leadership, but I would've been ready. My husband and I had decided in advance that we wouldn't accept 'no.' It was basically me saying that I'm taking this sabbatical, and so let's work together to make it happen. I went into the conversation with the target of taking a sabbatical in three and a half months. I ended up taking my sabbatical in six months, due to us needing to work through the transition and everything. Those six months were easier because we all knew my end date at work."

"Key things for me during the process were a supportive husband, a well thought out plan, predetermined options, and a supportive boss. I was very clear to communicate to my boss the reason for the request, which I think we should provide because companies or company representatives worry that sabbatical is code for 'I don't like my job anymore, and I want to find another one.'"

"I explained that I was having various health issues and needed to take time off to address them and then would return, that I really needed some time for myself to figure out what's going on, and that I would love to just have some quality time with my kids because they're growing so fast. Once I put a human face on the sabbatical, the support was immediate. I realize though that not everyone will have the support I had."

"Even if you hate your job, don't let your lead-in be 'I hate this place.' That usually doesn't go over very well. I think it's perfectly acceptable to explain that over the course of a forty-plus-year total career, it's very natural, at some points along the way, to need a substantial break."

Jade's comments got me and other collabHERators thinking more about breaks inserted during a stretch of work, or even during a stretch of learning. For example, during the first twenty-something years of our life when most of us went from primary school, to middle school, to high school, to college, there were three-month summer breaks, multi-week winter breaks, and a week-long spring break.

College professors take sabbaticals.
Athletes get an off-season.
Actors are on hiatus from taping.
Military forces personnel take leave.

In the corporate arena, what do we get? I'll tell you what we get. We get the wish factor. *I wish I could take time off, but I can't afford to* (again, not in the monetary way). If we do take time off, most of us settle for a two-week counterfeit vacation in which we're still putting in the work and can't fully separate ourselves from the office. We think we can continue at the same pace continuously without a reset. Some of us snatch the opportunity for a reset when we transition to a new job. We agree on a start date for our new job by building in a few weeks or longer for ourselves. During those weeks, we experience a much-needed break because we shut down everything from the old job, and the new one hasn't started yet. Zero baggage to carry.

I agree with Jade that it's unrealistic to think that we won't need an extended break. A genuine break. If we're in tune with our life rhythms, we can figure out our off-season and create a win-win around that. We might not secure a year-long sabbatical or even a three-month sabbatical, but we can make an impact on our well-being by being more deliberate about our weekends, our evenings, and that hour we might have to ourselves.

When You're in Overachieve Mode... Get Over It! Tips and Strategies

1. Decide what is good enough and what needs to be more than good enough.

2. Practice delegating in small steps and progress slowly from there.

3. Institute a daily pause that gives you space to just be.

4. Woo you! Embark on a love affair with yourself.

5. Stay true to who you are with small reminders of what and who bring you joy.

6. Give yourself periodic breaks during the day to do something for just you.

7. Start using nondual thinking. You're not either a success or a failure; you'll succeed in some areas and fail in others. Be okay with that.

8. Take a personal day and do no work.

9. Engage in an activity or hobby for which you have little to no skills.

10. Schedule rest on your calendar and keep the appointment.

Reflection Questions

1. Why do you think some women push themselves to achieve at any cost?
2. What is most important to you and why—success or significance?
3. What message do you send to your loved ones when you overachieve at work?

* * *

Do-Over Challenge

Although we may have heard that Sunday is the day when presumably most heart attacks occur due to the dread setting in of having to return to work, have you ever wondered why Monday is the most hated day of the week? In addition to Monday being the first day that most people drag themselves back to work, the day represents getting sucked back into our patterns and habits of work that we may likely resent. The more we lack a sense of balanced living, the more we tend to loathe Monday and all it represents.

Think back to a recent Monday morning that you dreaded prior to its arrival and then dreaded even more when it arrived. Consider all sources for the dread and list them. For example, a Monday morning meeting for which you used the weekend to prepare may be stressing you. Or maybe it's returning to your long, soul-sucking Monday commute. Or maybe it's the anticipation of that look in your preschooler's eyes when you drop him off at school. Or maybe, you flat out hate your job or your psycho boss. Don't worry about whether you have control over the source, just list as many as you can remember. The more specific, the better.

Sources of dread for Monday, [insert date]

1. _____

2. _____

3. _____

4. _____

5. _____

You deserve a do-over. Once your list is complete, write the word "ALL" next to each source over which you have control. Write "SOME" next to each source over which you have limited control. Write "NONE" next to each source over which you have no control.

For each of the "ALL" sources, come up with at least one way to eliminate the dread. For example, one of your "ALL" sources might have been the hustle and bustle of your family's morning routine. One way to eliminate the morning chaos might be to institute a predictable, predetermined breakfast for everyone, thereby cutting out time wasted figuring it out in the moment.

One of your "SOME" sources might be the Monday meetings at work. That it's Monday may not be flexible, but perhaps the time of day is. You could move it to a different time of day or make it a conference call which you could possibly conduct from home.

Your "NONE" source might be your commute. Instead of using the commute to fill your mind even more with the anticipation of what lies ahead, lift your spirits and move your emotions with music. Create a Monday playlist of tunes that you sing along with (if you drive) or that you privately groove to via headphones to help elevate your mood and energy. Choose an upcoming Monday when you'd like to put at least one of your ideas into place. On your mark, get set—happy Monday!

* * *

Make-Over Challenge

Courtesy of Jade, married mother of two

"During my sabbatical, I developed this new gratitude mindset. I focused on the things about the company I liked. I wrote them down. Things like travel, learning opportunities, and amazing individuals are some of what I put on my list."

"Because my sabbatical gave me the chance to both reset my personal state of mind and reflect on the good things about the company, it changed my focus. It changed my mindset about the organization. So, when I came back more energized to make a difference and to be part of the solution, I wanted to be a positive contributing leader, but also maintain my sense of self and sense of calm. I've been able to do that, and I credit, to a large degree, my gratefulness mindset."

You deserve a make-over. Like Jade's experience, practicing gratitude can be a game-changer. It shifts what the brain focuses on.

Grab a journal or a blank piece of paper. Create a list of all the things you like about your company. The only rule is that you have to come up with at least one. Reflect on this list daily at a time you believe is most advantageous (i.e., the night before work, the morning before work). You might even decide to reflect on it several times while you're at work!

Chapter 7

OVERcommit

"Somebody once said that we never know what is enough until we know what's more than enough."
— Billie Holiday

"Just because we can do anything doesn't mean we should do everything."
— Unknown

"Saying 'no' can be the ultimate self-care."
— Claudia Black

"Can you tell them?" they implored me.

After leading a session, on managing through change and transformation while being expected to take on more despite shrinking resources, for a mixed group of individual contributors and managers in Belgium, I was approached by a group of five women who wanted to speak privately. They were very careful to wait until the meeting room had cleared of participants before speaking.

While I was listening to their concerns and their subsequent request of me, it hit me. They don't fear that their voices won't be heard. They fear the consequences of speaking their truth.

"You are an external trainer. You have more freedom to take a risk and say the things we want to say, but don't feel that it's safe to say to the powers that be. Please make them understand that we are stressed and overwhelmed. There is both external and internal pressure to overcommit ourselves beyond what we can bear and not burn out. We want a life. We want to stay healthy. We also want to feel respected."

> **Get Real**
> The commitments on my calendar make me feel accomplished, make me look important, needed, and valuable. I'm so stressed and overwhelmed. I'm tired all the time.
> — Kristen, a collabHERator

Women are feeling the increased external and internal pressure to take on heavy burdens that we're not meant to carry. Often, we grow weary from the expectations, the long hours, and the amount of work to be done—all while blurring what we are doing to ourselves. Our batteries run dangerously low. We lash out at our company and our manager because we need something and somebody to blame. In the meantime, we try to plug into an auxiliary, superficial power source such as a grande dark coffee to jumpstart each morning. Our company and manager are not innocent in all this, but neither are we.

> **Get Real**
>
> I'm mad about the shift in power. Remember all the power that workers used to have? Now corporations have all the power, and they've been able to get away with stuff. You dare not say anything and be the lone voice because corporations have a whole slew of lawyers that would come after you and squash you and destroy your entire life. People are scared, and I totally get that. I understand that. Even HR can't be trusted because it's still an arm of the company. These hotlines where workers can call in anonymously with an issue, I don't trust them. No thank you.
>
> — Cleopatra, a collabHERator

The Art of Saying "No" with a "Hell No" Spirit

Can you jump on a call this morning?

Would you read over this client report to ensure that it captures all key points from our meeting?

We've all been there. Feeling overstretched by last-minute requests at work. Some of us may cite several reasons for saying "yes" even though what we really want is to say "no." And actually, sometimes saying "no" may be necessary for preserving and safeguarding our well-being in the midst of an already heavy workload.

Imagine the difference an arsenal of various ways to say "no" would make. Having a ready "no" available could help prevent becoming overwhelmed and overworked, while at the same time avoiding the discomfort and awkwardness of delivering a blunt "no." Try these out: "That won't be convenient for me," "I'm uncomfortable with that," or "I have a more pressing priority right now."

> **Get Real**
> I don't let a false sense of loyalty keep me from making the right decisions for me. I'm in my late twenties and have changed jobs five times. If I determine that people are crazy with unreasonable demands, I leave. I don't do crazy. There is no salary high enough to convince me to do crazy.
>
> — Crystal, a collabHERator

Rhonda, a self-professed adrenaline junky, insists that overachieving and overcommitting are related. "When I'm in overachieve mode, I work feverishly and on deadline. I get consumed and sucked in and lose perspective such that I say 'yes' to everything. The adrenaline high makes me feel invincible. It also shuts out every other thing. Achieving those goals and meeting those commitments becomes the most important thing in the world to me."

"The feeling of accomplishment and the resulting acknowledgment and recognition that come with it are exhilarating. The feeling is short lived though when I realize how much it costs. It's like a magnified sugar high followed by a magnified sugar crash. Sadly, this awareness doesn't stop me from doing it all over again. It's a cycle that's hard to resist. I look to activities outside of work that are exciting, enriching, and renewing to help manage this. Guess what? I bought a motorcycle. So not prim and proper! [laughter]"

> **Get Real**
> I pay attention to my physicality. If I start getting headaches or if I start having a lot of neck or jaw pain, it's my way of knowing that I'm falling back into old patterns.
> — Adrienne, a collabHERator

> **Get Real**
> My whole thing is to not get into a situation that won't be right for me. Worst-case scenario is I get myself in that situation, so then I think about how I can get myself out quickly before I am sucked dry. Some women I know have stayed where they are for twenty-five or thirty years. They're miserable and deal with so much crap. It's their own fault for staying and not saying anything. Some of us though, the younger ones, can get in there, assess things, and say, "Meh, this isn't it."
> — Jessica, a collabHERator

Contributing to the cycle is the underlying "what if." In other words, if I say "no" to what's asked of me, what if I lose my job? Valerie, an unattached forty-something-year-old and an only daughter among six male siblings, has an interesting take on this. "First, saying 'no' usually comes with a compelling reason and should open the door to dialogue and compromise to create a win-win situation. If my 'no' is met with the loss of my job, then it's a job I don't want. I think when a woman says that she can lose her job for saying 'no,' it's a perception thing that she wants to believe. A cop out."

> **Get Real**
> "Hell yeah, it felt good! When I quit, knowing my last day, I got progressively better and better, happier and happier.
> — Quinn, a collabHERator

Valerie asserts, "I have never myself nor have I met anyone who reports that her manager says she must take a call or lose her job. We take on this tremendous pressure to say 'yes' and then justify it by saying we have no choice. And we don't necessarily say it out loud. We internalize it and can get sick. That's what happened to me. The company or the job didn't make me sick. I did it to myself. I willingly walked into the fire. I stepped into the belly of the beast."

> **Get Real**
> I have a reputation as the go-to person. I created that reputation myself by my actions on the job. Outside of work, I reinforce that reputation. On the weekends, I'm consumed with the stress of family commitments. I make sure everything is taken care of and everybody is taken care of. Nobody asked me to take on this role. In my mind it's what I'm supposed to do as the woman of the house. So much goes unspoken and un-talked about, and then it becomes a tradition. It becomes a pattern of behavior that you don't question because it's what you know. It's what you do. Until your pattern gets interrupted.
> — Tracy, a collabHERator

"I have always wanted to run a marathon." This is the response I got from Isla, a fitness enthusiast, when I asked her about unfulfilled personal goals that have been sidelined in favor of priorities not her own. Not having fully recovered from a long-term illness, she offered some insights.

"Now that I'm getting healthy, I'm focusing again on running a marathon. If you were to ask me what stopped me from pursuing this goal earlier, I would have told you that I had to get the kids to soccer practice and do all the tactical things. I forgot the real picture. I get so involved in the day-to-day of life, whether it's the work deadlines and deliverables or the things that must be done for my family, such as playing taxi mom when my kids were a young age. No matter how far we've come as women, I know there's still a very big component of us that still feels like we are givers and nurturers. That's what we do."

"Neither my husband nor my kids demanded anything of me. I also don't remember anyone insisting that I stay home and rest or have a weekend just for me. Even if they had said it, I don't know if I would've done it. Maybe it's in our DNA. I don't know. I just think there are still so many mixed messages. There's so much I want for us women to have, but there's so much that we have to get past in order to get there."

> **Get Real**
> It probably wasn't until I took some time off and had my sabbatical that I became more introspective, prayed more, and sought counsel of others. I've seen a therapist, and she's been very helpful in asking me some little questions that have helped me identify the things that I do and then how I can control the situation differently. She helped me to see this whole idea of the standard I set for myself and how I hold myself accountable to things that I don't need to.
>
> — Jade, a collabHERator

> **Get Real**
> I overcommitted myself because I wanted to be liked. I wanted to be accepted. Like many women, I have grudgingly accepted that overcommitting doesn't leave me fulfilled. You eventually realize that the person or the things that you are going to extremes for, is never satisfied. They want more, and yet you're burned out and unhappy.
> — Monique, a collabHERator

> **Get Real**
> I have a bad case of FOMO [fear of missing out], so I try to squeeze in one or two more things even though I'm already exhausted. I'm afraid of falling behind everyone else, so I stay at least one step ahead. I'm afraid of disappointing people, so I agree to take on something I'm not interested in. I'm afraid of not being perceived as a team player, so I agree to accompany the group even though I'd rather be somewhere else.
> — Amber, a collabHERator

Putting Wisdom into Overdrive

Consider that we can go into overdrive to achieve goals that may not even be our goals, but rather goals that have been set for us. When they are at odds, should work goals ever supersede our own life goals? When they differ, should we prioritize work goals over what we really want for ourselves?

> **Get Real**
> Early in my career, I saw a female executive have a nervous breakdown. That memory has stayed with me

> and reminds me that it's only work. I have to honor how I feel and not let anything get in the way of that.
> — Camille, a collabHERator

CollabHERators in their mid-forties and above share a certain wisdom that comes from trial and error. Many insist that it took years for them to reach a certain realization around self-empowerment, prioritizing, and safeguarding their well-being. Does it necessarily take years for a woman to get to that place? If so, what are the implications for millennial and gen Z women coming up in the workforce?

Alejandra, single mother of a teenage daughter, thinks that young professional women can be in a place at the beginning of their careers and act on this wisdom. "They will get it from their parents because many do look to their parents. For some it's a positive experience to emulate and for some it's an experience to avoid. So, either way, they are getting a message from their parents. I work with many millennial women who watched their parents be miserable and work themselves into a fit. They watch and see their parents' experiences. They learn the lessons early."

"I still remember the day I received advice from my millennial colleague, Haley. Our meeting organizer was in the process of setting up a series of conference calls, each starting at 6 p.m., our time, to accommodate our global partners. Shortly after the meeting invitations came through, Haley came over to my desk and informed me that she had declined the call series and that she encourages me to do the same. Her rationale was that if our expertise was required, then it should be on a timeframe convenient for us. The lesson for me is that it's up to me. I must establish my own parameters and boundaries. Younger women are getting this early on and saving themselves much heartache and regret."

Regret is unproductive. Instead of telling ourselves what we should do or what we should have done, I believe in discovering who we are so that we can decide for ourselves what's right for us to do. What we do matters, but who we are matters even more.

> **Get Real**
> I now wish I had children, because I realize I have enough love to share, and the work doesn't truly fill the void. My journey is still before me, but I take it with a lot more caution, pleasure, and care. Today, I am cancer free, unable to have children, and have found love in the right place. My void has been filled with a true awareness of who I am. I've learned to love myself enough to know when to say "no."
> — Salome, a collabHERator

> **Get Real**
> My organization ran fine before I got there, and it'll continue to run fine when I'm gone. That's how I keep my perspective. I set boundaries around taking care of myself. We have to do that, and we have to start early with sports or exercise or meditation and prayer—whatever our suite of tools are.
> — Gina, a collabHERator

To be boundaryless means focusing so much on being giving and unselfish that we forget our limits and limitations. Setting boundaries is critical for health, well-being, and wholeness, thus impacting every part of our life.

The New R&R: Reprioritizing and Resetting

One of the best ways to guard against overcommitting is not just saying "no," but mastering the art of "no." The payoff is that we'll slow the frantic and frenzied pace and we'll resist the urge to add more and more to our schedule. Overcommitting is not a badge of honor. There is no way to maintain priorities when we overcommit our time and energy.

> **Get Real**
> A friend and I were just talking about overcommitting. I gave her your book when she was here visiting. We were having that age-old conversation where she said, "I'm trying to do this, this, this, and this, and I'm trying to move up in the company." She's remarried with three kids and two step kids. She said, "Lately, I've been thinking about what you've always told me. "You can have it all, but you can't have it all at the same time."
> — Wendy, a collabHERator

Though we say we want them to, our values don't dictate our actions in some areas. Why is it that in spite of our deep desire for more balanced living, we continually make the same mistakes of taking on too much and overdoing it? Why do we continue to cling to disempowering patterns of behaviors that don't serve us?

Megan believes that "stress makes us stupid. It's the same principle behind why men can be so dumb and clueless in one area and brilliant in others. We share that in common. Stress activates our excuse-making, blaming, procrastinating gene."

> **Get Real**
> I don't want to be *that* woman who doesn't have her shit together.
> — Toni, a collabHERator

Not fully knowing the seriousness of our situation may be our body's way of protecting and insulating us. That is, until matters reach crisis level, and then the physical stuff kicks in to get our attention.

> **Get Real**
> Cancer taught me that life is not promised, and I must pay attention to my body. Most importantly it taught me that I must make myself a priority. So today, I truly have it all. I still work hard, but I also take care of myself. I continue to be plagued by my weight, but I make sure I drink water, and take downtime. I no longer see honor in working all night because my nights are not promised, so I must cherish each one.
> — Salome, a collabHERator

> **Get Real**
> I have a soft spot...a tough spot for new moms. It's one thing to overcommit ourselves when we are single with no romantic attachments and no children. But new motherhood changes everything, even more than a life partner does. Think about it. You can't do all of the same things. You have this little person you're taking care of that depends on you for everything. It's just hard to do. So, yes, it doesn't feel good to say "no," but does it feel better to let down your baby? Your family? You have to say "no." Your "no" can be "not now" or "here's another

> resource" or "here's a different way." However, sometimes your "no" really is a "no" and should be.
> — Octavia, a collabHERator

Rest Is All about You

The physical, emotional, mental, and spiritual costs of overcommitting are very high. Fatigue is not just a one-dimensional issue. It hits from all angles and permeates throughout our entire being. Physical fatigue can manifest as an exhaustive burnout that isn't easily remedied by a good night's sleep. Emotional fatigue can activate the short fuse leading to negativity and irritability. Mental fatigue can result in poor focus and lack of sustained concentration. Spiritual fatigue can leave us vulnerable and susceptible to misaligned values.

> **Get Real**
> It's called mind-body-spirit connection for a reason. Paying attention to the mental and spiritual parts is the bigger piece of it, but it's what happens to the body that gets our attention. One of my close HR colleagues in the UK suffered major burnout. She had to leave work for a while. She was experiencing major breakouts and massive migraines from the stress of being so overwhelmed. She was running herself into the ground. That was all physical. But before all that happened, she said that she had grown miserable in the job, she just wasn't happy, and she wasn't satisfied. She just kinda sucked it up and stayed with it. That to me is mental and spiritual stress. It was her red flag that she dismissed. People have their reasons for staying in situations that may not be best for

> them. But yeah, that physical stuff will stop you in your tracks.
>
> — Bethany, a collabHERator

Based on my own experience and the experiences of my collabHERators, by the time stress manifests itself in our physical body, it has already gone through our mental and spiritual channels first. We're so busy and so distracted though, we brush off the warning signs or we suck it up and continue to power through despite unhappiness, misery, overload, etc. We think we can keep going when mind and spirit are diminished because nobody can readily detect what's going on with us. At least that's how we rationalize it. We haven't processed the real seriousness of it.

We say to ourselves that we can keep going when in reality we're operating with limitations. And even if our best friend at work knows or suspects something, it's not obvious to everybody else so we keep pushing through. On the other hand, if we're sitting crumpled in a meeting with a crushing migraine and our face is jacked up with hives and rashes, then that's going to be obvious. As Bethany says, nothing gets our attention quite like a physical symptom. And what of our mantra before it struck? *I'm a can-do Betty. I'm a high achiever. I get stuff done. I get results.* Well, Betty just got taken down by a migraine and a rash. Game over.

When it comes to healthier lifestyles, sometimes we need to rewrite our own narrative in this area, one that honors mind, body, and spirit. For example, if we know overdoing it makes us prone to overeating and weight gain or undereating and weight loss, what this means is that we have a compelling reason to eat right and exercise. We have an opportunity to build and sustain healthy habits for the long term and leave a legacy of a healthy lifestyle with our family and friends. And for the pain of migraines or skin conditions or unexplained mystery illnesses, what this means is we'll get good at seeking and securing help from doctors and other health care practitioners to manage the stress impacts to our body.

When You're in Overcommit Mode... Get Over It! Tips and Strategies

1. Practice different ways to say "no" without apology.

2. Delegate.

3. Focus on only what you can control and devise strategies from there.

4. Establish clear boundaries and limits, write them down, and review them regularly!

5. When you sense you are about to overcommit, say "stop" to yourself.

6. Schedule time with yourself and keep it!

7. Put a limit on daily commitments, track it, and hold yourself accountable.

8. Rework a commitment you don't want with one you do.

9. Team up with a support and accountability besty with similar challenges.

10. Play hooky from work for a day and do anything you want.

Reflection Questions

1. Where have you not established boundaries where you need to?
2. When have you said "yes" when you needed to say "no?"
3. How have you put yourself last when you should have put yourself first?

* * *

Do-Over Challenge

You deserve a do-over. We can sometimes get so one-sided in our perspective that we immediately default to thinking that we must "do" in order to "get." Suppose instead that you can "let go" in order to "get."

Think about the commitments you currently have. These would not be the mandatory commitments related to you or your family's basic needs of food, shelter, or clothing. List three commitments you'd like to ditch.

Create your list with no guilt or self-condemnation. Once you look at your list of three, choose one and start developing a plan to make your ditch-dream a reality. Move to the next one until you have a plan for ditching all three. Let the thought of what you'll gain by letting go motivate you during the process.

The only thing left to do is to put your plans into action!

Theresa M. Robinson

Make-Over Challenge

Courtesy of Cassie, an entrepreneur who left her corporate career of twenty years

You deserve a make-over. Take a lined piece of paper and fold it in half the long way. On the left side write down everything you said "yes" to today. For each yes, what did you have to say "no" to? Write that down on the corresponding line on the right side.

"This exercise is amazing because a lot of times people find that everything they said 'yes' to is just the stuff on their to-do list. And on the 'no' side, what's revealed is that by spending more time on my to-do list, I didn't have dinner with my family or I didn't make it to my kid's rehearsal or I didn't get enough sleep, or I didn't take care of my body or I didn't eat healthy food."

The point of this challenge is not to say that to-do lists are intrinsically bad. The idea is to shift our perspective so that instead of looking at our to-do list and feeling like the tasks are screaming at us, it's about being more deliberate about what we're going to say "yes" to and what we're going to say "no" to. And saying "no" may mean "not now" or "not today" or "delegate" or "scratch that all together."

Women especially can be prone to having a hard time saying "yes" to ourselves. Cassie and many collabHERators agree. "It is super hard for me to say 'yes' to me, but when I do, I find that I'm so much better at everything. Oh my gosh! You have to experience it, but you have to do it first to experience it."

Chapter 8

OVERaccommodate

"You can never leave footprints that last if you are always walking on tiptoe."

— Leymah Gbowee

"You can be a good person with a kind heart and still say 'no.'"

— Lori Deschene

"It's easy to think that people will like you more if you do whatever they tell you to do, but it's quite the opposite."

— Osayi Osar-Emokpae

The breakup wasn't easy.

I ended it with a "no."

And it was years in the making, after a consistent stream of "yeses," which took the form of me overaccommodating to please and satisfy in a relationship that felt more like "give, give, give" above and beyond on my part and "take, take, take" to put profit above people on the part of the other.

I broke up with a company.

Here's what happened. My love and passion for the work had outgrown the relationship. Whereas my values clearly steer toward prioritizing people over profit and process, the company subscribes to different priorities—a not-for-people, but for-profit code of values. Whereas I look at trust and communication as core anchors in any relationship, the company binds its relationships with fear and control. Whereas I seek to be valued and appreciated for my contributions, the company fosters an environment whereby its people feel unvalued, underappreciated, expendable, and easily replaceable.

Such a lack of mutuality. The other party is benefitting way more than you are, and yet you are a big reason they are benefitting. It's not right. Have you ever had those moments when you just know it, you just feel it?

Get Real

I did the same thing you did. My values no longer aligned with the organization's values and culture. It wasn't me that changed. The company and its leadership did. I know exactly what you're saying. When we're no longer comfortable, our choice is to change our values or change the company.

— Val, a collabHERator

I'd say that nearly everyone to some degree has struggled with insecurity, fear of rejection, or the fear of not being liked or accepted. There is nothing inherently wrong with wanting others to like us, but when we are so focused on being people pleasers to the point where we start overaccommodating to the detriment of our own wants and needs, then that signals an issue. Ask yourself this question: "Is my overaccommodating nature hijacking and controlling my choices?"

> **Get Real**
> Doing the right thing can cost us. Sometimes the cost is losing a client account. Sometimes the cost is needing to quit your job because to stay means compromising or giving up your values.
> — Jin, a collabHERator

Apologizing Too Much

Imagine what can happen if women confront the "I'm sorry if this sounds [fill in the blank]" preamble. Shannon, a recovering please-aholic, knows exactly what can happen. "I used to be the one in team meetings to express my ideas or opinions with an opening apology or other tentative intro. I started picking up on how this caused the people on my team to view me as timid and how this translated to how they treated me."

"That's the thing about apologizing so much; it sends a wrong message. I'm different now. I say it and act now and, if necessary, ask for forgiveness later. It has done wonders for my confidence, and my team seems to have a newfound respect for me and my ideas."

> **Get Real**
> Overapologizing can become part of a pattern, and people can now start to predict we'll always do it. So, if we're constantly apologizing no matter what form it takes or whether it's actually using the word "sorry" or whether it's through more subtle forms, people's perception of us is going to change. People lose confidence in our ability if our responses or results start with "sorry" all the time. An apology signals an admission that we did something wrong or did something not great. We lower others' expectations of us for the future. We lower their regard for us. Men don't make apologies. They should sometimes. But they don't. I can't think of any male figure from my career where I could point to him and say that he apologizes too much. I can point to Suzy though and accurately predict that she'll preface what she says with apology.
>
> — Fiona, a collabHERator

Being overapologetic takes many forms. It's not just the example from Shannon's experience or the literal "sorry" from Fiona's comments; it may be the apologetic stance we take regarding ideas themselves and how we position our ideas. Maybe we have an idea about which we feel strongly, yet we want to control the perception that we are too assertive and not a team player. We pose the idea as a question rather than a statement.

What does everybody think about [insert idea]?

Semantic nuances like this are how many of us couch our ideas to soften them and make them more palatable. At the same time, these strategies may be hiding fear issues. *What if people think my idea is stupid? The less I seem vested in my own idea, the less stupid I will appear.* These strategies may also be covering up for confidence issues. *What if I have no idea what I'm talking about in this area? If I turn it into a "we" thing at the start and not a "me" thing, I won't take the sole hit.*

Giving Away Our Vacation

In addition to putting our vacation plans on the backburner in favor of accommodating business activities or the competing vacation preferences of colleagues, we sometimes trade our vacation for a pseudo vacation in which we continue to work during what amounts to a vacation in name only. We can take back our vacation with this unconventional, no-holds-barred OUT OF OFFICE NOTIFICATION.

> *Hey. Psst. You and I both know there is no such thing as "no access to email." There is ALWAYS access. But here's the thing— I am away with my husband and two kids on an amazing family vacation that we've been planning for quite some time. I'm sure you can imagine how priceless it is for us to get away, so we can connect with each other and create some incredible memories. I pledged to my family that I would completely disengage from work and be totally present, so I will not be checking email or voicemail at all. Again, not checking. Really. If, however, your matter is truly urgent, and you need my assistance, here is my husband's mobile number: 281-555-5555. Call him and run your emergency by him first such that I might gain his support and forgiveness for violating my promise due to your emergency. I will*

be back in the office fully recharged and ready to get back to work on November 13.

Trying Too Hard to Accommodate

Does each of us know where to draw the line at distinguishing between flexibility/adaptability and overaccommodation? Do we even know what never makes sense to try and accommodate in the first place? Early in my career, I didn't.

Once, after facilitating a session, I received the following written feedback from a participant.

"I was overwhelmed by her eyes. So big, and they seemed to get even bigger at times. I felt like I couldn't get away from her eyes."

Green and eager, I was devastated and vowed to take action before my next session. When the day arrived, I felt confident that my eyes would not be an issue for anyone in my audience. I had worked so hard to make adjustments to accommodate for the possibility that even one participant might comment negatively on my eyes. And I wanted so desperately to please.

So, imagine my shock in reading not just one comment, but many comments echoing the same sentiment.

"Great class. Couldn't figure out though why she kept squinting at everybody."

My lesson learned: in my zeal to please, I had resorted to unnaturally forcing my big, expressive eyes to get smaller and, in the process, had done a great disservice to myself and the participants.

Get Real
I don't know how to make myself happy, but I'm always the one making other people happy or comfortable. I greet
---

> people at the office in the morning. I'm the one most likely to bring in doughnuts. I plan and organize our office parties. I'm the one asking if anybody needs anything. I feel like if I don't do it, nobody else will. Even as a child, I was the pliable, obedient one who played nice by the rules.
> — Blair, a collabHERator

Putting on the Brakes

Sometimes it's harder to stop something than it is to prevent it in the first place. Joining a new team gives us a fresh start and a new opportunity to determine how we'll operate and how we'll communicate it to others. Jade's philosophy is that at the beginning we have to train people how to treat us because they honestly might not know.

> **Get Real**
> I had just relocated to Canada and was working with a new leadership team, and it was the day of my first meeting with the team. My manager was a male, and so was everyone on the team. I was okay being the only woman. I'm used to it. What I wasn't used to was my manager approaching me before the meeting to say, "I'm hoping that you'll take the notes during our meeting." I could have easily been accommodating as the new person on the team, but I said, "I don't think that's a good idea." He was shocked and taken aback and responded, "What do you mean?" I said to him, "I'm the only woman on the team, and I'm your HR person. I don't want my role to be reduced to administrative tasks. I'm happy to take the notes if we rotate so that it's not just me and so that we're sharing the responsibility among the team. Or we can have an assistant come to the meetings to take the notes."

> He stood there looking at me, and I was imagining he was thinking that what in the world had they just gotten themselves into by bringing me onto the team. Because he still wasn't saying anything, I kept going, "Of course I will not be insubordinate if you decide that my taking notes is what needs to happen, but I think we should unite and come from a different place than where you're coming from." He came over to my way of thinking with a simple, "Okay."
>
> — Jade, a collabHERator

Jade further revealed that as she got to know her manager better, they looked back at that initial incident and discussed it within the context of having grown more comfortable and at ease with each other. She discovered that her manager had thought so highly of her organizational skills, that he felt she was the only one who could do justice to the role. She is quick to point out that she's not making excuses for him or men in general, but we tend to view men in the workplace as if that is all they are. However, these are men that may be coming to the workplace from homes with traditional gender roles in place.

She stresses, "There are men I've worked with who had wives that work at home. Their wives manage the household and the household schedules. That's what some men live, so then when they come to work, I don't know if they're able to make that shift. And I have to be honest with you; there is something to how ingrained these gender behaviors become, not just in men, but also in us."

Jade made me think about my own household. I travel a whole lot, and because I do, I've told my husband that I don't clean house. And guess what? Neither does he. Over the years, we've had several cleaning ladies (a term he and I both use that might be problematic, even though each cleaner we've ever found has been a woman) that clean our house on a regular basis. Always a cleaning lady. Never a cleaning man.

My husband believes that it's my domain to research and find a cleaning lady, schedule her, and pay her. It hasn't been worth the energy to fight him on this, even though every now and then, I might say something out of sheer annoyance at having to do it all the time.

Another reason I don't fight him on this is because I made a similar declaration when it comes to trash. My position is that if I'm the only woman in a house with a husband and an adult son who are both physically stronger than I am, why should I be the one taking out the trash and the recyclables? Sometimes I deceive myself into thinking that my rationale is more about physical strength than about gender, but even if I were the strongest, I still wouldn't take out the trash.

I. Am. Not. Doing. That. End of story.

Household dynamics and workplace dynamics can get very tricky. Women and men occupy both spaces. So much of what persists in households stems from gender role conditioning. My husband comes from a strict, traditional gender role upbringing. Mine was a patchwork upbringing due to being raised alongside two sisters by a single mother. Every household responsibility was carried out by a female: cleaning, taking out the trash, doing the dishes, washing laundry, washing the car, raking the yard, cutting the grass, etc. We were even taught at a young age to change a flat tire. At the same time, external sources made it very clear to me and my sisters what the gender expectations are.

How much of it all does each of us take into the workplace? And how much of it should we not take? None of it?

> **Get Real**
> By the time I got to the workshop session, there were no seats left. Several men were already standing against the wall. I'm sure it showed on my face how tired I was and disappointed to have to stand in a packed room. As I looked around, there was a man I didn't know motioning for me to take his seat. I quickly walked over, thanked him, and sat down. He joined the other men standing against the wall.
> — Chris, a collabHERator

Cracking the Language Code

What if we did away with the interviews in which companies put on their best face and instead create an environment of brutal honesty so that candidates know exactly what they are getting into?

Consider the following hypothetical interview between Mary, a hiring manager, and Christine, an applicant for a marketing director position. Christine has just asked Mary about the culture.

Though Mary doesn't say it, what if all signs pointed to this kind of response. "Our goal is to work you to death and squeeze every ounce of contribution out of you. Be prepared to miss out on many family events."

According to Pam, a human resources professional, there are several coded questions that we can ask during the interview phase to gain insight on the culture of an organization we're considering joining.

"Of course, there are certain types of information that can't be shared. Even if you ask those kinds of questions, the good news is that the interviewer will likely provide what I call a consolation prize answer. Without violating any rules or protocols, the interviewer may still inadvertently provide you with some valuable insights. So, if you want to assess turnover, you can ask about the tenure of team members in a certain department/division. To assess diversity and inclusion, you can ask about gender distribution in certain roles, about the existence of employee resource groups, and advancement opportunities. To assess the value the company places on its people, you can ask about health and wellness initiatives, training and development opportunities, and flexible work arrangements, etc. Finally, you can ask whether the company conducts regular employee engagement surveys of its people and what things have been implemented as a direct result of the surveys. If any of the responses to these questions raises a red flag, run, and run fast. It will save you tremendous headache and hardship."

Get Real

So many of us talk a good game. Men, too. We say we put our family first before the company. Yada, yada. That we prioritize our values over the company. Yada, yada. We're all really good at saying those words. We need to learn how to model those words.

— Sasha, a collabHERator

**When You're in Overaccommodate Mode...
Get Over It!
Tips and Strategies**

1. Stop apologizing so much.

2. Get very real about the distinction between compromise and surrender.

3. Is there a positive WIIFM element? (What's in it for me?) If not, rework or abandon?

4. Treat you like you treat your best client/customer.

5. Confidently express your needs.

6. Choose more discriminately between minimums and maximums.

7. Implement a balanced give-and-take philosophy.

8. Start journaling your needs and wants.

9. Set priorities and limits.

10. Create an affirmation that you say to yourself when you feel susceptible.

Reflection Questions

1. Who and what are most important in your life?
2. Where are you going above and beyond to make things more convenient for others?
3. What are the costs to well-being, relationships, and joy when women consistently place others' needs and wants ahead of their own?

*　　*　　*

Do-Over Challenge

It's difficult to take a long hard look at all the costs of wanting to accommodate and please others, especially if we think that our behaviors will lead to our acceptance. Sometimes it's easier to stick our head in the sand than confront the truth about what we do to ourselves. However, until we confront the "me," we won't be motivated enough to want to move past it all.

You deserve a do-over. Think about the most recent example of how you went out of your way to accommodate the needs of another. Complete the statement below about the incident.

The primary reason why I _____

was because _____

Make-Over Challenge

You deserve a make-over. Are you in need of a powerful way to ensure that you stop accommodating others at your expense and start prioritizing YOU? Do you need a way to hold yourself accountable that takes less than five minutes to set up?

Try this. At the start of each day, write this question in a journal and answer it:

"What will I do today that is just for me?"

Then at the end of the day before you retire for the night, pull out the journal and turn to the same page where you wrote the earlier question and your answer.

Now write this question and answer it:

"What did I do today that was just for me?"

Nothing is too small when it's something you do just for you. Try it for a week as an experiment and tell at least one person what difference it makes.

Chapter 9

OVER Isolate

"I'll be honest with you. I'm a little bit of a loner. It's been a big part of my maturing process to learn to allow people to support me. I tend to be very self-reliant and private. And I have this history of wanting to work things out on my own and protect people from what's going on with me.
— Kerry Washington

"Sometimes the girl who is always there for everyone else needs someone there for her."
— Bianca Sparacino

"I can do things you cannot, you can do things I cannot; together we can do great things."
— Mother Theresa

The sign is clear. "No bikes allowed on trail." The park where I like to do my power walks has two trails: one very scenic and peppered with shade trees and the other more pedestrian. Both however, are for walkers and joggers only. On this particular hot, humid, and sunny morning, I and another walker had chosen the scenic trail. She was some yards ahead of me and was accompanied by her daughter who looked to be about four in age.

Both were the object of dirty looks by passersby. The four-year-old was on a bike and was not doing a good job of steering it or staying out of the way of others on the path. She was like a mini drunk driver, weaving in and out of the path and then slamming on her brakes only to trip up the person behind her. I was walking in the same direction as the woman and her child, but because the direction one could take on the trail was flexible, I could see the looks of annoyance and irritation on the faces of those who passed them. She saw their faces as well and was doing everything she could to keep her young daughter from crashing into oncoming joggers.

She kept repeating, "I'm sorry. Oops! So sorry!"

As I was overtaking them myself to pass, she met my eyes with a look I'll never forget. Her words were, "I'm sorry," but her entire facial expression seemed to convey to me her story. At least that's what I chose to believe.

Here she was, perhaps a struggling single mother or perhaps not a single mother at all, committing to her health and well-being. Maybe this was the only time of day that she can exercise and there's nobody to watch her daughter. Perhaps letting her daughter ride her big girl bike was the only way to avoid one of those epic, toddler-like tantrums, one of those Britney Spears kinds of meltdowns in the parking lot. I remember those all too well. My heart went out to her and to whatever her situation might be.

Each time I lapped her, I gave her an "I've been there!" smile and said, "It's okay." I wanted her to know that there are times when we can't go it alone and must rely on the kindness of a community of strangers to get us through.

Beth relayed a story regarding the "no children" rule at certain places and insists that these situations raise a dilemma. "When should the support needs of others outweigh my needs? I understand why the "no children" rule is put in place. Sometimes for me the "no children" spaces are the only places where I can go and feel like it's my space for some peace. Going to a spa or a fitness class is my Independence Day, and I get a bit resentful when kids are brought in despite the rule. I've already put in my time with my own kids, who are much older now. I don't want to deal with somebody else's kids. I'm done."

> **Get Real**
> I feel refreshed and uplifted when I can walk away from my life for a few hours to spend time with my women friends in a no-men and no-children zone. Wine and commiseration equal good times and generate so much laughter. My friends give me and my situation perspective. I feel like a new person when I return home.
> — Dara, a collabHERator

What Are We Trying to Prove and to Whom Are We Trying to Prove It?

The issue is not that women can or cannot do it all by ourselves. The issue is that we don't have to—for whatever reason. Plus, every woman's definition of "all" is different relative to her own circumstances and desires.

> **Get Real**
> See, here's the thing. Women talk about support, and how we're such the collaborative gender. We talk of sisterhood, support systems, our bond. Blah, blah, blah. We all do it. But then when you look at a lot of us, we're so super independent and standoffish. We have our noses stuck so high in the air or so far up our own asses.
> — Kim, a collabHERator

According to Victoria, remarried after losing her first husband to a long-term illness, "It's like we think we can do it better or that nobody will be able to take care of things the way we take care of things. We actually make things harder on ourselves at work because we don't delegate. And we make things harder on ourselves at home because we shame our partners, who we insist can't do things to the same standard as do we. When my husband died, I let go of my control and perfectionist tendencies. Watching someone you love suffer and being powerless to do anything humbles you and drives you toward the help and support of others."

"Over independence and self-reliance isolate us. When we cut ourselves off from others, especially other women, we can't give help or receive help. Alone time is good, but I know of a practical way we can prevent isolating ourselves for so long that it becomes detrimental." (See Victoria's make-over challenge at the end of this chapter.)

> **Get Real**
> The biggest lesson I learned was never be afraid or ashamed to ask for or pay for help.
> — Antoinette, a collabHERator

A Word about Delegating—Yes, Again

Delegating. Though its benefits are often touted, we all have our reasons for not doing it. Each of us already knows everything I'm about to say, so why am I saying it? Because some of us still don't get it. Maybe the umpteenth time will be the charm. When we fail to delegate, we'll wear ourselves out. Think about the workload of the office and home. It's too heavy for us by ourselves. If it weren't, we wouldn't be complaining about being tired and exhausted and not having time for things we'd like to do.

Trying to do everything ourselves is a bad form of leadership, and we're all leaders with the ability to impact and influence those around us. Lack of delegating leads to the underutilization of other people's skills and talents. We can't grow people if we're not allowing them to exercise their gifts and explore passions. They'll grow frustrated, and so will we. Once we get clear on the win-win of delegation, we'll wonder how we ever survived without it.

Being a Safe Haven

Thanks to social media, people seem more connected now than ever before. However, outwardly we can appear to be close and unified, when in reality some of us feel isolated. New mother Debbi elaborates on this sentiment. "As a professional woman, I look to accomplished and established women as mentors, guides, and role models. So many of them are hating on millennials though. It's ridic! I want women in my network where I can feel mutually respected and understood. I want to share my wins and failures. I want affirmation and validation. I don't want to have this generational difference stuff hanging over our heads to divide us."

Less Is More

We live in a world that tells us to climb higher, make more money, accumulate possessions, seek power, forego substance, and rely on substances. However, none of these was cited by collabHERators when I asked what they need most in their life. In no particular order, here's what we want:
    Self-acceptance.
    Fair treatment.
    Love.
    Healthy relationships.
    Happiness.
    Romance.
    Fair pay.
    Peace.

Pride and Pretenses

Pride may goeth before a fall, but first it'll isolate the hell out of us. Isolation prevents us from being vulnerable, and it's hard enough to be vulnerable without the added challenge of isolation. It can be too risky to leave ourselves open to hurt, harm, and betrayal. Not many of us are willing to sign up for that! Because we're being judged all the time, we want how we see ourselves and how others see us as having it all together. We work hard to maintain that image. Perception management. The higher our career level, the higher our wealth, the more high stakes is perception management. With that kind of burden, consider how hard it is for us to admit that we feel like we're on the edge or too overwhelmed to cope.

> **Get Real**
> There are some things you can't say to certain people, but I want to make that conversation more okay. I'm trying to find more people who'll have that conversation. I started looking closer at the people at work and my guess is that 60 percent of them are on depression or anxiety medication.
> — Angie, a collabHERator

> **Get Real**
> My mother tells the story of me at age two always insisting, "I can do it all by myself." Now all these years later, I am that stubborn and petulant two-year-old still saying it.
> — Crystal, a collabHERator

We Don't Outgrow the Need for a Village

We tend to over isolate ourselves even though we understand the power of what happens when we all can come together and help each other. For many of us that's how it used to be during our childhood. Megan, who recently became a grandmother, looks back on this and compares it to today. "Everybody in the neighborhood knew you. You were one of the kids in the neighborhood. All the parents were just as involved in setting you on the right course as were your own parents. As a neighborhood kid, you could be nurtured and chastised by any adult living on the block. Everybody helped each other out. At the time, I didn't realize how lucky I was to have that kind of communal support."

"Now we put up walls. We build barriers. We separate ourselves from what we need most. The more affluent we become, the more we close ourselves off from others. We go to work all day. We drive home, push a button, and pull our car into our garage without even setting foot outside our door. We then push the button again. The garage door closes behind us, insulating us inside while keeping everyone else out. Because there is no contact with our neighbors, you can arrive home having lost your job, and nobody would be the wiser. When I look back at my pattern of behavior, I realize that the more responsibility I was given at work and the more money I made, the more I isolated myself from a support network. Affluence has a way of doing that."

Help me? What? I don't need help. Thank you very much.

As Megan points out, isolation isn't about not having proximity to others. It's possible to be isolated when around many people. Isolation is a lack of connection stemming from various factors. Megan references affluence as a contributing factor. When we succumb to "affluenza," we can grow susceptible to self-imposed quarantine and block out others from getting in. Maybe we fear that others will judge us, misunderstand us, or betray us. We might withdraw even further, threatening our current connections because we're so consumed by our independence and our busyness in proving ourselves.

Over isolating ourselves is a vicious cycle. When we isolate ourselves, it's difficult to ask for help. But when we can't ask for help, we continue to isolate ourselves. Karyn, in her late forties, insists that she knows one thing for sure that breaks the cycle. "When something major in your life happens that is beyond your control, you can no longer isolate yourself. Being diagnosed with cancer was my wake-up call."

"You learn first to accept offers of help, which eases you into being able to ask for it. Now that I look back, I went from thinking that I wouldn't need help to accepting help to welcoming help to asking for help. Cancer gets the credit for my heightened awareness that self-reliance is detrimental when taken to extremes."

Needing and asking for help do not imply any moral failing on our part. No one expects us to do life alone. We don't have to. But sometimes it takes a huge shift in our circumstances to remind us that we are communal and relational creatures.

For Karyn, it was cancer, clearly a life-altering event. For Tess and Gabrielle, it was the birth or adoption of a child. For Suzanne, it was the death of both parents. For Victoria, it was the death of her husband. For Brynn, Elaine, Jane, and Tricia, it was the breakup of a marriage and the subsequent change in status to "single mother." The common thread around being able to seek out and accept support and help appears to be situations and circumstances that we can't control.

Get Real

As I lay in bed crying, on the third day after I threw my husband out after fifteen years of marriage during which he hadn't worked and had gambled away $250,000, I realized what my priorities were. While he had been staying home raising the kids, they were not doing any sports, doing any music, having adventures, or being encouraged to be social. Isolated from the world, their expertise was channel surfing. Not something to be proud of. These kids were going down the exact same path as their self-absorbed, narcissistic father. I realized that if I wanted to create change, I was the only one who could

> make it happen. And with that realization, I dried my tears, gritted my teeth, climbed out of bed, kissed goodbye the perfect marriage fantasy, cleaned the shower, signed them up for rugby, football, private music lessons, put in three loads of washing, and arranged dinner with friends!
> — Jane, a collabHERator

Control issues. CollabHERators and I confess them and claim them. We've also laughed at ourselves because of our paradoxical acknowledgment that releasing a need for control is freeing. We know ultimately nothing good comes when control issues go rogue. Wendy, who jokingly refers to herself as a charter member of the control club, insists, "Women have a need for security, so we try and exercise as much control over stuff as possible because it gives us that sense of security we may not be getting anywhere else."

When situations we can't control come along, they shake us up to the core and disrupt our security. Whether it's the cancer diagnosis or the end of our marriage, we are forced out of our patterns.

Get Over Yourself, Get Outside of Yourself

Our tough circumstances can make us self-absorbed. We are so much in our own heads, that body and spirit become collateral damage. At an overachiever level in which we're so driven, we self-isolate even though we may have a partner. And even though we have friends, we have moved away from them. Overachieving creates distance and separation. Our mindset can grow disconnected from body and spirit, without which we lose touch with the importance of supportive relationships.

> **Get Real**
> I have friends I trust who cheer me up when I'm sad, who calm me down when I'm mad, who make me laugh, who tell me I'm wrong or I'm being stupid.
> — Kara, a collabHERator

If we pause and think about it, it's hard to get things done in isolation. Additionally, if we're in a leadership position in which we're not willing to ask for help, others could perceive that as our unwillingness to bring people along or the unwillingness of others to join or share in what we're attempting to do. The danger is that once we become known as the person who doesn't seek help, it may make others wonder if we believe in help. That could lead to others not approaching us when they need help. It can lead to a culture of isolation with people working in silos inside a vacuum. This creates more work stress for us, because we'll be struggling and can't even tell anyone. Have you ever felt like you had to suffer in silence? If so, that may be a sign that you are a member of the "go it alone" tribe—a vast and growing membership despite no known benefits.

> **Get Real**
> I had my support circle of girlfriends that gave me advice. It was one of those girlfriends that said to me, "Hey, Jade, you oughta take some time off." She made real what I already knew. Her words gave me the courage to talk to my husband about taking extended time off from work. And then with his support, I put the wheels in motion. That support circle is so important.
> — Jade, a collabHERator

Stop Being a Selfie

It's not as easy as a click and upload. Being a selfie means that even though we can only step back so far, we think our limited perspective provides our best shot. It can take serious effort to break the go-it-alone mode. It's both good and bad to be independent, based on how independence manifests itself in our relationships and in our interactions with others.

To go it alone is not brave. Isolating ourselves can be very lonely. We may not realize the extent of our loneliness because of the overwhelm and overload of busyness. No woman wants others to know how much she's really struggling, so we continue to isolate ourselves and try to solve our problems on our own.

> **Get Real**
> I've had to bite my tongue with my husband to avoid saying to him, "I don't ever want to have to financially depend on you." I don't want to embody the myth of the strong, independent black woman, but I'm carrying that baggage.
> — Kristen, a collabHERator

Change is hard. Change is also doable at any stage and at any age. One of the reasons we fail at sustaining change might be that we take the pressure off of ourselves. Without pressure, we revert to old familiar patterns whether we like them or not. The relapse or quitting is just a part of the problem. The other part is that we've ignored all we've learned and achieved. Lasting change ideally should be reinforcing and self-perpetuating.

> **Get Real**
> I seek advice, and I value the incredible network that I have access to. Based on that input, I make my decisions and relish in the power of living the life that I now choose for my children and myself. I may question my own decisions, but no one else does. Recently, my tax agent criticized me for my financial investments...so I sacked him, on the spot. How dare he! The freedom that comes with living on our own terms and pursuing our own priorities is our reward. Life may still be busy, but it won't drag us down unless we let it because we have the power to change it.
> — Jane, a collabHERator

> **Get Real**
> What has helped me to wean myself from going into autopilot is having a small tribe of accountability partners: my mentor, my life coach, and my younger sister. Each gives me a reality check about the value proposition of going into one of my "O" modes. They call me out on my shit because that's what I need to have harmony in my life. It's a daily journey, but I've learned to appreciate the power of being "in the moment" in my own life and for those that share my world.
> — Monique, a collabHERator

> **Get Real**
> If you really want to change, you have the power to do that today.
> — Lisbeth, a collabHERator

Sure, we can go solo, but why would we if we don't have to? Interdependence. We can lean on the support of others during stressful periods, we can bask in their encouragement when we're sad and frustrated, and we can benefit from their guidance on the way forward. It feels so good to have people in our life with whom we can be real and laugh and cry.

When You're in Over Isolate Mode...
Get Over It!
Tips and Strategies

1. Forge friendships with women in similar positions.
2. Join a social group or online chat group.
3. Ask for and accept help from family and friends.
4. Plan a girls' night out or a girls' vacation.
5. Put the same energy into building your personal network of support as you do your professional network.
6. *Be* with the people you're with.
7. Practice HALT: don't get too Hungry, Angry, Lonely, Tired.
8. Set a personal goal impossible to achieve alone.
9. Volunteer at a homeless shelter.
10. Perform a random act of kindness for a neighbor at work or at home.

Reflection Questions

1. When do you feel most isolated and alone?
2. What is the best thing that could happen if you admitted a desire or need for help and support?
3. How do you model an open-door policy at work?

* * *

Do-Over Challenge

You deserve a do-over. You wave to them whenever you see them at the mailbox or whenever you both are pulling your vehicles into the driveway. They are the neighbors who live next door, across the street, or perhaps two houses over. You've never officially met them and don't even know their names. The odds are, they don't know yours either.

Before we can love our neighbor, it helps to first know our neighbor. Do you know your neighbors? If not, how can you change that? What one thing can you do this week to start building a relationship with your neighbors? Get out there.

Make-Over Challenge
Courtesy of Victoria, remarried after her first husband passed away

"Try this experiment. Be intentional about connecting with people. Go to the grocery store and be kind to every person that you come in contact with. When somebody drops something, pick it up for her. If somebody in the line behind you has only a gallon of milk, and you've got a full cart, let that person go ahead of you. Maybe you'll spend an extra five minutes in the grocery store, but you can handle that. I promise you that you're gonna change at least two people's lives—yours and somebody else's."

"When you quit isolating yourself and quit walking around like a victim, and do something, *you* change. Things change. You can't be both kind and isolated at the same time. Choose kind and watch what happens."

PART III

What We Want from Allies

"There comes a time in your life when you can no longer put off choosing. You have to choose one path or the other. You can live safe and be protected by people just like you, or you can stand up and be a leader for what is right. Always, remember this: People never remember the crowd; they remember the one person that had the courage to say and do what no one would do."

—Shannon L. Adler

Chapter 10

Not Every Woman Has Your Back

"I learned a long time ago that little girls compete. Women support. They don't play victim or snipe at each other. Strong women stand tall and deal."
— Areva Martin

"There is nothing worse than doing nothing and saying nothing when your voice is needed."
— Soledad O'Brien

"Be a woman other women can trust. Have the courage to tell another woman direct when she has offended, hurt, or disappointed you. Successful women have a loyal tribe of loyal and honest women behind them. Not haters. Not backstabbers or women who whisper behind their back. Be a woman who lifts other women."
— Sophia A. Nelson

I was crushed. All signs pointed to me. I had tenure, experience, great client feedback, etc. But no. She told me to my face that for this major assignment with wide exposure and visibility that she had decided to go with John, my less-tenured, white, male colleague that I had helped train. When I inquired why, her response blew me away because she and I knew exactly what she meant.

"You don't have the universal appeal that John has."

Translation. Most of our clients are white males. John is a white male.

As the VP of training, she was the final decision maker on all matters related to training delivery.

I was speechless.

Sensing my shock, she proceeded to try and smooth things over. "We both know how this works. It doesn't really mean anything. You're one of our best facilitators. You understand, right?"

She actually thought she was making it better!

Still no words from me.

"You understand, right?" she implored.

Oh, I understand all right. It's as clear as day. So clear, I can see right through you.

"Theresa?"

Stop talking. Please stop talking.

To save her life, I simply walked away and never mentioned it again. My image of her from that day forward was permanent ink stamped across her forehead with the words "woman card revoked."

She had violated the unspoken alliance and support of a sisterhood, a group of women who, experiencing similar injustices, make it a point to advocate for and advance other women when in a position to do so. What she had done was to sabotage me while perpetuating an unfair system.

Whether she was maliciously deliberate in her intent or blissfully ignorant of her complicity was of no consequence to me. The impact on me remained the same.

> **Get Real**
> Remember when Robin Roberts, [*Good Morning America* host], made that on-air dig [December 14, 2017] to Omarosa [Manigault] when she said, "Bye, Felicia?" She got some criticism for that from people who were shocked that she could be so unprofessional. I was cheering though because she said out loud what many black people, particularly black women, were thinking. Omarosa single-handedly did so much to damage the cause of black people and the cause of women. Too much stuff to go into, and so when Robin said what she said, it was the perfect send-off! I still laugh about that moment.
> — Denise, a collabHERator

Rival, Adversary, or Foe

No surprise. Women are subject to envy, judgment, unjust criticism, and unfairness from other women. We know it when it happens. We feel it when it happens. It's instinctual. According to Dara, in her thirties and a sorority member, "Women can distinguish the difference between a woman that has our back and one that is out to sabotage us. For instance, when something good happens at work and people celebrate us, some women will fake celebrate and you can feel it. The combination of the feeling along with how they gush is what tips me off. 'Oh, my God! I'm so happy for you!' Yeah, fake."

That feeling that Dara describes is echoed by several collabHERators and is cited as what allows us to keep our guard up and be wary.

> **Get Real**
> When my mom was in town, she met me at my office, so we could go to lunch together. While she was there, I introduced her to several of my coworkers, several of whom are women. Afterwards at lunch, I looked at her and asked which of the women is pitted against me. I already knew, but I wanted to see if she knew just from first impressions. She didn't even hesitate. "The one with the short brown hair nearest the window." She was right. When I asked her how she knew, she said, "Her words didn't feel right to me, and she gave off a vibe when she shook my hand." That feeling we have is a gift. When we don't pay attention to it, it can sometimes get us into trouble because we don't see something bad coming, and then we say we were betrayed. I strongly believe in women's intuition, but I think in some cases we just ignore it. As women, we want to always look for the best in people. We want to give them a shot because we want to be optimistic.
> — Maya, a collabHERator

> **Get Real**
> The fact that more than half of all white women voted against Hillary Clinton shows one of the insidious ways patriarchy puts women in competition with each other. That the term "frenemies"[4] refers exclusively to relationships between women is another way.
> — Victoria, a collabHERator

---

[4] The term frenemies refers to two or more people who pretend to like each other and get along, but below the surface there is a rivalry perceived by all parties.

Quite frankly, I've met some women—and men, for that matter—over the years, who gave me such a bad feeling inside that I found it necessary to abandon my get-to-know-you-better strategy and run fast to avoid them. Unexplainable, yes. Real, also yes. I listen to my spirit. If a new acquaintance sets off screaming alarm bells, I listen. I remain cordial, but distant, and proceed with caution. If I feel in my spirit that someone who has been a friend or acquaintance now means me harm, then I start the process of "lovingly" releasing that person from my life. The stronger the feeling, the quicker and more blunt the release process! Whether we call it spirit, gut, intuition, a feeling, a vibe—we may be doing ourselves a disservice if we dismiss it too quickly without first closely examining the source to which it points.

> **Get Real**
> It's the women. Definitely, it's the women you have to worry about more. In my industry, there are a lot of powerful women which is great. Some productions have an all-female creative team, which is really cool to see and empowering. But on the other hand, if you want to climb up the ladder and there's a lot of women on the ladder, sometimes they're not your advocate. The women sometimes are the ones that you have to watch your back for.
> — Ashley, a collabHERator

According to Merriam-Webster's dictionary, a rival is one of two or more persons striving to reach or obtain something that only one of them can have. An adversary is described as one that contends with, opposes, or resists. And a foe is someone who has personal enmity for another.

Though these definitions don't seem to fully and accurately capture my experience with the VP of training, they do a good job of pointing in the direction of what my collabHERators describe as some women's need to compete with and put down other women by any means necessary.

Have you encountered them? Women detractors who seem to revel in undermining us? Women who seem to live by the mean girl playbook from middle school? Who seem to make a game out of making themselves look good at our expense? When the behavior of a woman detractor reaches a critical point, some of us might avoid her or shut down. Others might strike back passive-aggressively to shut her down. Still, others might copy the behavior with others.

There are no words to convey what it feels like to be thrown under the bus by another woman. Sadly, there are certain things women have come to expect from men because that's the world in which we currently live. But when these same things originate from women, it's a totally different feeling. It feels like betrayal. And it cuts deep.

Some collabHERators postulate that unhealthy competition is fostered in some women due to women's exposure to highly competitive environments dominated by highly competitive men. Further fueling the competition is that some women subscribe to the idea that there can ever only be one or few women allowed in certain positions. The gender quota fear. Token women.

Other collabHERators point to unchecked comparison and the rise of jealousy as the root of unhealthy competition between women. Often, it's women's own insecurity that keeps us looking at other women, longing to be who they are and have what they have: smarter, thinner, more patient, more successful.

It's critical that all women get this. One woman's success doesn't take away from another woman's success. One woman's skills and talents don't diminish another woman's skills and talents. If we ever get worried that another woman will outshine us, look to the sky and consider the stars. They're countless and all shine, making the entire night sky a magnificent sight to behold!

> **Get Real**
> There are women in leadership roles or otherwise who don't support other women because they are threatened by them. Therefore, they talk over other women, etc. It's as if they have to be the smartest person in the room. Thankfully, there are less and less of these women, but some still exist and don't have the confidence to let others shine. They don't support other women who may be viewed as smarter than they are. I experienced this recently as this woman said to me, "There isn't room here for the two of us." She has to be the center of the conversation, and if that means stopping women from speaking who she perceives to be smart, she will use her position of power to try and stop them by overtalking them and using their ideas as her own. The other related aspect of this is when you're interrupted or talked over and there is an attempt to use your ideas by stating them first. You sometimes question yourself as to whether you should speak up because it's your female boss and there may be real repercussions.
> — Lynn, a collabHERator

Oh No She Didn't!

As a facilitator I'm always super thrilled to have women in my sessions, because of the instant bond I hope we share. Though I work with all-women groups and all-men groups, the mixed-gender groups tend to have very low female representation.

I remember one occasion when I led a session of all men and one woman. Let's call her Betty. Because I know what it feels like to be the "only," I pulled out all the stops to ensure that Betty felt included and that her voice was heard over any potential overtalking by the male participants.

In looking through the evaluations at the end of the course, imagine my reaction in reading through her comments, which she believed would be anonymous, to discover that she had provided the following piece of feedback about me, "Trainer needs a pedicure."

Seriously?! That's what you want me to know?! That's what you got out of the session?!

I knew the evaluation was hers because all the other participants had chosen to put their names on their evaluation forms. And their feedback was mostly glowing and positive with a few pieces of relevant and helpful constructive feedback (i.e., "give more time to discuss X before the activity" or "shorten the review of Y"). None of their feedback was personal in nature. This judging stuff is a double-edged sword. Men may see us one way, and women will judge us in another.

It still saddens me that in all the years I've been doing this work, the most brutally personal and irrelevant feedback I receive is usually delivered by women. My female colleagues who work in learning and development agree. I asked some of them to share with me some of the most mean-spirited feedback they've received which they know came from women. These don't even represent everything. There were more than these. I've tried to give an idea of the full scope of women's critical eye by highlighting these literal head-to-toe observations.

Too thin
Too fat to teach wellness
Bad hair weave
Too dressed up
Dressed too casually
Not enough makeup
Too much makeup
Lipstick on her teeth
Kept playing with one of her earrings
Bra straps showing
Pit stains under her arms
Sleeveless blouse inappropriate for work
Blouse too low cut
Skirt wrinkled
Dress too short
Stain on front of her pants
Hairy legs
Heels are inappropriate for business

> **Get Real**
> I hate to be that person that says, "You hate me because I'm pretty." I hate to say shit like that. I absolutely hate it, but I really do feel like some women feel threatened by how you look or how you carry yourself.
> — Simone, a collabHERator

Yes, there are certain aspects about a facilitator that could be distracting for participants. However, if personal comments are the only focus or the primary focus to the exclusion of feedback of substance, we have to consider motives. Plus, we can tell when a woman is looking for something to pick apart. Do we formalize similar critiques about a man? Though we may notice, do we point out his armpit stains, his black shoes with brown pants, the coffee stain on his tie? And as a consequence, do we downgrade his performance or pronounce an indictment against his performance? No.

Do some women feel better about themselves when they can tear other women down? It's one thing for a woman to make these critiques inside her head, but it's another thing for her to then formalize the critiques and make them publicly available on a written evaluation.

Most training participants know that evaluations are reviewed not only by the facilitator of a learning session, but also by stakeholders. Many others are privy to evaluation data. With participant Betty likely knowing this, why would she feel a need to try and publicly shame me? I don't know if I have an answer for this. This goes beyond being "catty." This is different. Within the context of the challenges women face from men, the additional affronts we face from some women add insult to injury.

Et tu, woman?

Get Real

I have a female assistant that I share with a female colleague. The assistant reports to both me and my colleague. I don't sit in the same pod with either of them. I sometimes have to go over to their pod for something. There are two other women in their pod, one of whom is always staring at me when I go over. She stops whatever she's doing and watches and listens to everything I'm saying to my assistant or my colleague. She's known around the office for gossiping. I can feel and see her out of the corner of my eye. That's already a red flag for me. I

> want to ask her, "Why are you watching and listening to the entire conversation instead of doing your work?" I don't feel like she's on my side and is looking for a reason to not like me. One day she said something inappropriate, and my thought was, "What the fuck?!" I had to turn and look at another woman and ask, "What did she just say?" And because she sensed my levels were getting high, she responded, "Don't worry about her." I shot her a look and loudly said, "Mm-hmm," and walked off. I'll be cordial with her, but I'm not going to pretend that she's not a fucking red flag now. I don't trust her, and I know she doesn't have my best interest. I'm a team player, but I won't go out of my way to help her.
> — Simone, a collabHERator

Whether it's justified or not, when the battle lines are drawn, there can never be a true sense of team. A mentality akin to each woman for herself makes that impossible. Rivalry and snarkiness foster separation. We retreat into ourselves and vow to not put ourselves at risk of getting burned again. Once we feel like something is personal, it can override any business imperative regarding the work itself.

As I think again about participant Betty, not only did she make her feedback personal, she made it a personal attack based on her judgment of what the appearance of my toes should have been in open-toe shoes. I'm sure no details escaped her. She had likely sat there all day with what I can only imagine was more eyes than ears. She had scanned me from head to toe, until her eagle-eyes landed on my shoes and then my toes. If the training had been more than one day, perhaps she would've also picked up on the fact that I had not shaved the tiny little hairs on the tops of my toes, which in my thinking I had never considered would be noticed or would matter.

For her to take the anonymous feedback route was the cowardly cop-out route. It was an "ouch" delivered in the spirit of meanness. Straight out of the mean girl playbook. If she had stopped to consider whether her comment was true, kind, and necessary, I'd like to think that she would have never made it.

Would we all think twice about the judging we do if we were to use this criteria?

Is it true?

Is it kind or helpful?

Is it really necessary?

If the answer is "no," to even one of those questions, then we'd best serve ourselves and others to simply back off. Though many judgments go unspoken, they can be used by the judger to make decisions that impact the judged in negative ways.

Ouch!

"Ouch." Unlike some four-letter words, this one can help instead of harm in that it creates a space for open communication to occur. Let me explain. As a diversity and inclusion catalyst, I coach teams on the use of "the ouch" strategy as a way to encourage dialogue through uncomfortable situations. For example, if a person is hurt, offended, or otherwise negatively impacted by a comment or action, she would say "ouch" in that moment. The immediacy and relative simplicity of "the ouch" can be very powerful as it opens the door for deeper dialogue around the offended person's perspective and feelings. And isn't that what this world needs more of—a greater awareness and understanding of others?

> **Get Real**
> Women need to come together even more to help each other. We need to look out for each other and be champions for each other. We're not being real champions for each other. When one of us is bold about who we are and what we want, women have to be more comfortable with that. At the same time, we have to be willing to say and do things that make people uncomfortable. What it's gonna come down to is that we have to do uncomfortable things and also say uncomfortable things to get the dialogue started.
> — Jennifer, a collabHERator

> **Get Real**
> The other thing I've tried to do more of as a woman is stand up for other women. I don't think we do that.
> — Hope, a collabHERator

Knowing the Right Moment for Confrontation

One of the hardest aspects in all this is knowing when it's the right time for confrontation. CollabHERators couldn't agree on a formula for determining the right time. Maybe it's just better to jump in whenever we feel it, regardless of timing. The time and place can help to dictate the "how" of the confrontation. Yes, it can be scary and can carry real consequences, but failure to confront others is in itself a choice that comes with consequences— both real and imagined. Healthy conflict, discomfort, and confrontation are rarely easy and rarely second nature, but they are critical in initiating dialogue, challenging the status quo, and righting wrongs.

> **Get Real**
> In the past, I've confronted women colleagues in private and cried "foul." I confess that I still struggle with calling women on their shit when I report to them or they have a higher position than me.
> — Angie, a collabHERator

The world in which we live is very complex with a diverse global citizenry with interests and agendas often at odds. In our lifetime, we will likely face many wrongs and injustices. Women who actively sabotage women disappoint us on such a deep level.

> **Get Real**
> The truth I don't want to face is that I'm more unsupportive of women than I think I am, more jealous of them than I want to admit.
> — Jill, a collabHERator

> **Get Real**
> Women need to be really careful about making sure that we hold ourselves accountable, too, because there are women out there that are powerful, and we overlook some of their questionable or inappropriate behaviors. We can't overlook that stuff anymore. We have to hold each other accountable and not give someone a free pass just because they're a woman.
> — Vicki, a collabHERator

> **Get Real**
> Misconduct and incompetence are gender neutral. Some women can be just as bad for the cause of women as some men are.
> — Jean, a collabHERator

Unintentional Mentor

When Valerie made the decision to leave her company, it was unheard of. Many people thought she was crazy. No woman who has worked so hard and achieved that status throws it all away. That was the prevailing sentiment. What Valerie recalls though are those who viewed her as brave. "Once word was out about my decision to leave, I had lots and lots of conversations, particularly with women."

"These conversations ultimately ended in my not saying much and listening to how miserable women were, how trapped they felt, how working at the company had made them feel like hostages, how they couldn't make a change because of this or that. I became a mentor by default, just by listening. I wasn't even trying to be a mentor at this point. Women were gravitating toward me because I represented for them the voice of realness."

REALationships with Women

Priscilla, a mentor for female youths, explains, "I can't remember where I saw the term, but it stuck. Realationships. R-e-*a*-l. I believe it was within the context of the lie that when a woman wins, another woman loses. The truth is that when a woman wins, women win."

Ironically, collabHERators of color understand all too well this principle because we live it in reverse. When a person of color does something wrong, it's not uncommon for all people of color to be condemned or implicated.

> **Get Real**
> A Latina who was on our team years ago—she's gone now—felt the pressure to make her numbers and forged a client signature on a contract to close a deal. To hit her target. They found out about it and fired her. From that point on, it was just us who were looked at real closely. Eight of us.
>
> —Tatiana, a collabHERator

According to Joyce, in her mid-fifties, "Women coming up don't have the wisdom or experience that older women have gained from dealing with this mess for so long. But we don't always have the fresh perspective and courage that they have. That's why it's so important that we share with each other. Support each other. This project is so important."

Beyond the demographics of age, collabHERators have commented on race, sexuality, and other aspects that differentiate us within the larger category of women. For instance, there are additional layers of gender inequity specific to women of color and LGBTQ women that are not shared by white women and which can't be given adequate treatment within the scope of this book. Yet, it's important to acknowledge and talk about these differences in identity and experience, and it's also critical to come together as a collective body that wants each woman to feel valued, to feel whole, and to feel healthy despite what might be going on out there. Whether we work for a crappy company or a good company, whether we work for a shitty boss or an awesome boss, our unity strengthens and upholds each of us.

> **Get Real**
>
> A community of sisters exists, but it's been unspoken outside of the community. It's been largely unarticulated. For example, black women who are at a certain place in our careers, we share so many commonalities. There are certain things that I know that you know, and we don't even have to say it out loud to each other. And because you and I know, how do we manage knowing that certain things may get said to us or happen to us? We have this commonality of shared experience, but at what point do we share it with other people outside of our commonality—this big unspoken thing—that we constantly have to navigate? I don't even know how to articulate the question? But it's complicated, and it's hard. This is not easy stuff. It's never been easy stuff. I can't judge somebody responding to a microaggression differently than how I would respond to it, because I don't know enough about that person's detailed experiences to that point or what they feel inside and how they cope with adversity. It may be the exact same offense I've experienced, but this person may respond to it this way, whereas I may respond to it that way. I'm not going to judge how you respond because I know this stuff is real. What's happening is real, because I'm a part of it, too. It's tough. It's tough. And it hurts.
>
> — Audrey, a collabHERator

Jeanine insists that before the sharing, there must first be relating. "I think we as older women have forgotten how to relate to younger women in the workplace. And sometimes this translates into unintentional sabotage or a lack of support. What I mean is that we can be just as unaware as the men at work when we're not supportive and understanding, say, for example, about childcare challenges. Imagine the impact if we simply said to our female colleague or direct report, 'How's everything going with daycare? I remember when I went back to work after my first child was born. I was a nervous wreck about everything.' That kind of relating opens the door to meaningful connections."

> **Get Real**
> I feel like I was missing a wise older woman in my life to give me some of that guidance as an adult. As a child I had a close relationship with my mother, but you know I'd say over the last ten years, our relationship has been more reversed where I find myself trying to be a parent to her more than she is to me. And so, it's interesting as an adult I feel like *I'm* my own mentor and I should be figuring all this out because other people have made all these things work.
>
> — Jade, a collabHERator

The good news in all this is that we can stop women detractors in their tracks and turn things around. We can do this by refusing to stoop to the same level and rising above their tactics with poised professionalism, by resisting the human inclination that tells us to repay injury with injury. When we can't get through to our detractors, we can go over them and around them. My mom taught us to attack our enemies with kindness because it's what they least expect, and so they aren't prepared.

Be so kind as to even figuratively nominate your female foe for an employee of the month award and watch her be shamed into remorse! We can become known for our integrity and sound work ethic. Trust me. Women detractors who insist on pursuing their course will be reduced to an old-fashioned "bitch-fit," as Toni calls it, when they see us flourishing and succeeding despite their efforts to the contrary.

**Not Every Woman Has Your Back...
Get Over It!
Tips and Strategies for Supporting Women**

1. Speak up and speak out in meetings where you see "it" happening.

2. Publicly commend the ideas and achievements of women to others.

3. Cross-mentor women in an earlier stage of their career.

4. Sponsor another woman.

5. Create a scholarship fund or sponsor an internship for women.

6. Groom a woman to take on your position when you leave or are promoted.

7. Foster friendships with other women, not just a working relationship.

8. Endorse a woman for an open position you know about.

9. Create a women's network or join an existing one.

10. Affirm women on their inner self and not their appearance.

Reflection Questions

1. How have you been sabotaged by women?
2. How might you have contributed to the unfair treatment of women?
3. How do your actions communicate to women that you support women?

*   *   *

Do-Over Challenge

From your past, think about any missed opportunities to mentor women with less experience than you. They may have been women you turned down when they asked because you were too busy and didn't have time. Or they may have been women you attempted to mentor, but you fell short. Or they may have been women who never asked, but you believe they could have benefited from a mentoring relationship with you. No matter the reason, you deserve a do-over.

Think about the present. Write down the names of at least three women to mentor. What names would you write and why? What could you offer to each of them? What benefits do you believe you'll receive?

Names of three women I could mentor:

1. _____

2. _____

3. _____

Now, come out of your comfort zone and approach at least one of these women in the next thirty days. Watch both her and you grow more enriched from the relationship.

* * *

Make-Over Challenge
Courtesy of Amber, self-described FOMO sufferer

According to Amber, insecurity and jealousy are the reasons women sabotage women. "We constantly compare ourselves to other women. Pure and simple. If we were to all admit it, we'd say that we've been just a little bit relieved to see a woman get passed over for the promotion that we also got passed over for. It's good to get to the source of that insecurity and jealousy, but in the meantime, try this. For me, I've found that gratitude instantly shifts my perspective, allowing me to slay the monster, which is me. It's like going from beast to beauty."

"It's a two-step process. The first step is truly humbling and eye opening. It's what I call confession." Complete the following statement:

I wish I had (a) _____ like hers.

"The second step is celebration." Complete the following:

Here's what I have: (List three things you're thankful for.)

1. _____

2. _____

3. _____

Chapter 11

Not Every Man Is Clueless and Action-less

"A woman has got to...[experience] a bad man once or twice in her life, to be thankful for a good one."
— Marjorie Kinnan

"The most basic and powerful way to connect to another person is to listen. Just listen."
— Rachel Naomi Remen

"But here's an important warning: you don't have to have mentors who look like you. Had I been waiting for a black, female Soviet specialist mentor, I would still be waiting. Most of my mentors have been old white men, because they were the ones who dominated my field."
— Condoleeza Rice

Every chapter to this point opens with a short piece designed to set the tone for the theme(s) to be addressed in the chapter. I knew I'd write this chapter last, even after the conclusion, because for months I've been racking my brain to locate an experience to recount in which a man, other than my husband, has ever spoken up or advocated on my behalf. I can't think of one. Not in the classroom. Not in a meeting. Not on the airport shuttle.

Ironically, the omission of a story does indeed set the tone for this chapter because there are not nearly enough men in this role.

If Men Would Only Shut Up and Step Up

"A woman who speaks up is not a bitch."

"A woman who expresses a different opinion from a man is not a bitch."

"A woman who is strong and states what she wants is not a bitch."

These are just a few of the many raw sentiments expressed by collabHERators. As Wanda put it, "When a man truly respects a woman's intellect, her capabilities, her drive, her accomplishments, there's no room for any insecurity. His precious male ego doesn't feel threatened. The default to 'she's a bitch' is a dead giveaway to what type of man he is. The minute he calls (or thinks) a woman a bitch—whether it's coded underneath words like 'combative, contrary, or aggressive'—he exposes himself for what he is: a jerk that needs a major mindset adjustment."

As several collabHERators pointed out, what's dangerous about these kind of men is that so many of them are in positions of power. They make decisions that negatively impact women. These decisions easily become de facto policy within already existing structures and systems that are unfair to women. A woman's potential for career mobility can often be a matter of how she's perceived and regarded by men. Does she know "her place?" Does she operate by "the rules?" Does she make our male customers/clients "comfortable?" Biased gender criteria such as these are oftentimes prioritized over our skills and experience.

> **Get Real**
> Women are conditioned to adapt to whatever and whoever is around them. Men don't know how to deal with a variety of women because we come in all styles, personalities, shapes, and sizes. There is no one size fits all for women, so no matter how men were raised and no matter their experience, they need to recognize that when they are out in the world, there's a whole spectrum of us. So they need to get to know us.
> — Regina, a collabHERator

> **Get Real**
> Change is about celebrating and being comfortable that no matter who you are, we are all different. I could be a pixie with pink ears, but get to know me and allow me to convince you I am capable and that I can excel. So, in the world of work just see everyone for what they can offer and measure yourself the same way. Never anything more. Utopia maybe. But maybe if we try this piece of simplicity, who knows…
> — Cindy, a collabHERator

Wanda continues, "For men to step up means they are real allies for women. These men are out there. Great. They may be reading this right now. Before they can step up, they must listen. And to listen, they must stop doing all the talking. We need more men to step up. One aspect of male privilege is that it can result in a lack of self-awareness. And ironically, if a man thinks he doesn't need to read this, the odds are that he does."

Male Privilege

> **Get Real**
> Have you ever noticed that it's always the benefactors of privilege that never want to acknowledge it exists and don't even want to talk about it? When it comes to white privilege, white people get pissed hearing about it. I know you've included white women in this project obviously, but even they get pissed hearing about how they benefit from white privilege. The minute the focus shifts to male privilege, now all of a sudden, they're on board and want to talk about it.
>
> — Kim, a collabHERator

That the subject of male privilege elicited many comments is no surprise. Cheryl's thoughts summarize some of the similarities in how collabHERators viewed men's responsibility around male privilege. Cheryl, married stepmother of three, calls herself a justice warrior. "Men need what I call burning moral courage. Some people would call this doing the right thing. But putting it in those terms is not strong enough. Burning moral courage comes with a strong sense of outrage."

"But you only get that sense when you are keenly aware of the extent of the injustice. Men have to be willing to listen and admit that they benefit from male privilege and that they knowingly or unknowingly allow it to continue. They also have to deal with their selfish tendency to not want to lose those benefits. It's easy to theorize about, but harder to do. In reaping the benefits from the gender gap, men can be expected to have an attitude of non-urgency about fixing it. Resistance and opposition can be brutal when it comes to righting things that have been wrong for so long."

"Look at the backlash of what's going on with Trump's base thinking they're losing their 'rightful place.' Though not many admit it out loud, the whole 'make America great again' is really 'make America white again,' and it's meant to reference a history of white privilege and power. That's the ugly legacy of this country."

Lindsey, a first-generation college graduate and the oldest of her siblings, agrees up to a point. "Making it primarily about race is short sighted. What about class? Plus, there are so many systems of oppression. I think that when we topple one—gender discrimination—then we can topple the others. Right now, we as women have to be focused on what unites us rather than get too distracted by racial differences. As a white woman, I know I benefit from white privilege, and I want to work on dismantling the system that allows me to benefit. At the same time, I'm willing to use my platform of whiteness to get more men to listen."

Get Real
Allies can be men or women. But men will be better because a lot of times they're often in positions of power to be able to help. I'm just a bit off-topic, but why is it that the LGBTQ movement seems to have accelerated, and acceptance has accelerated at a pace so much faster in some ways than making things better for women of color or people of color in general? The theory is because most people now have someone that they know who's LGBTQ—

> whether it's an immediate family member or friend or kid of a friend or somebody. So it's no longer what I see over there that has nothing to do with me. It's over here now and it's a personal issue that I can relate to and identify with because of somebody I know and love and care about who is experiencing discrimination. If you're white, you're probably less likely to have a black or Hispanic or Asian person in your family or inner circle that you really love and care about. So, it's harder to empathize with the inequities that exist. For white men to support women of color, it's not personal enough to them, and it doesn't impact them personally. For men of color to support women of color, they're not powerful enough. They are just as disenfranchised as we are.
>
> — Hope, a collabHERator

Hope is not as off-topic as she thinks. Explaining the business case for gender equity is one-dimensional and incomplete without a compelling personal appeal to the heart. When an issue doesn't touch us personally, we are less likely to view it as an urgent call to action. A prerequisite to men acting as allies is them experiencing a change of mind and a change of heart. It's not enough that the business case for gender equity and inclusion makes sense in a man's head; it has to also travel to his heart.

Getting men to see and understand how they would want their daughters to be treated is a primary focus of gender strategist, Jeffery Tobias Halter. Bringing men on as allies, advocates, and champions must make personal sense as well as business sense. Some men have stay-at-home wives and may be old-school traditional in their lifestyle outside of work and unable to imagine a wife in an equal role in the workplace. However, if they have a daughter, they may be able to see her as somebody who can ascend to various levels of leadership. It's an innovative hook. Jeffery's initiative is called *Father of a Daughter Initiative*. It has yet to gain the needed critical mass of men to make a substantive shift in the way things are for women, but what Jeffery is doing in this space is very admirable, as the initiative seeks change, one father at a time.

> **Get Real**
>
> I hate it when men say, "I'm a dad now, so I see women differently." Why did it take them now having a daughter? When they preyed on women or disrespected women, didn't they have a mama the whole time? How were they seeing it then? Whatever. That doesn't cut it for me.
>
> — Simone, a collabHERator

Allies have to create accountability because that's how the culture will change. It starts with leadership. Mike, a consulting group principal, underscores the importance of the role leadership has in this. His example also highlights the good that happens when others in a position of power push back. "Amanda had just come on board six months ago. It was evident how incredibly knowledgeable and engaging she was, and so when there was an upcoming opportunity to have her deliver a series of presentations for a key client group, I knew she'd be perfect. The client's top decision maker, however, didn't think Amanda would be a good fit, that she didn't appear to be a team player, and that she didn't have the right skillset."

"However, I strongly believed in Amanda and knew she'd be brilliant with this professional audience and stood by my choice. I defended Amanda and lobbied for the right to make Amanda my choice as I strongly believed the outcome would be the best thing for this client group. The decision maker relented, and Amanda delivered with rave reviews."

Mike could have simply decided to keep the peace and not make waves with the client, but he decided to staunchly support her, and today he insists that "Amanda has my support every time, no matter what the situation." Mike took a risk in losing a client account because he believed in Amanda and her skills.

It didn't matter that the client had provided a series of vague rationales that are often used to squeeze women out. Mike saw past that and pushed for Amanda. Imagine the multiple gains from this scenario. Amanda knows she is in a supportive environment where she is valued and prioritized over misguided clients with unfair attitudes toward women. The client knows that Mike employs stellar talent on his team and that it's best to trust his judgment. Because of Amanda's phenomenal delivery, it may also go a long way in busting existing gender bias within the client's organization.

Get Real

When a leader is in place who demonstrates what he or she cares about, it's evidenced by the promotional decisions they make, where they show up, and how they spend their time. Are they willing to meet with groups of women and talk to them about their issues and concerns, and then do they take action to address those issues? That says a lot. And when you have the highest leaders at the highest level doing that, it changes the expectation of leaders below. I think that's the biggest way to change the culture. You know what gets rewarded and recognized. If you're not promoting the guy who's the primary offender

> of women, that says these behaviors are not acceptable. If you're promoting the person who is for equal opportunity, that communicates what the company values and rewards. It really comes down to leadership accountability and what the company rewards and doesn't reward. I also like to see who's getting demoted and who's staying where they are. All that is part of the big picture. Each of us has individual accountability to be the voice that leads to change.
>
> — Beth, a collabHERator

Ask, Listen, Watch

Communicating value to anyone, not just to women, is about wanting the other person to feel known, heard, and valued in a way that's unique. Many collabHERators agree that if men are intentional about engaging in uncomfortable conversations with women, it would make women feel safer. Women might reveal more of our true selves. It opens a door for both sides to be able to answer and ask difficult questions.

> **Get Real**
>
> If I could give one piece of advice to all men, it would be this: get outside of your own male privilege and be more others-focused.
>
> — Pat, a collabHERator

Can Men Learn to "Speak Woman?"

Many of us can agree that women have had to speak both man and woman. We've had to. I wonder what men even think it means for them to *speak woman*. No matter what we think about it or how we feel about it, women know what it means to *speak man*. In a lot of cases, it's how we've managed to navigate male structures. Imagine if more men became "multilingual" in this way and learned to speak woman. Can they?

> **Get Real**
> Straight up, the only men I know that can speak woman are gay! [laughter]
> — Melissa, a collabHERator

Brad, an ally, thinks men can learn to speak woman. "In my personal life (marriage) and professional life, speaking woman equates more to listening than speaking. Men tend to be 'fixers' and therefore they wind up jumping in and speaking, before they hear the entire story. Being raised in a family with sisters as well as having an amazing wife, I have learned that men cannot fix everything, so just listening has been the best way for me to speak woman.

> **Get Real**
> I love the concept of multilingual for women…Meryl Streep said recently, "It's like women have learned the language of men, have lived in the house of men all our lives. We can speak it. You know when you learn a language, you learn French, you learn Spanish. It doesn't really become, isn't your language until you dream in it. And the only way to dream in it is to speak it. And women speak men. But men don't speak women. They don't dream in it."
> — Katelyn, a collabHERator

> **Get Real**
>
> Men separate themselves from what's going on around them. Clearly that stereotype—you know, the one about how they want to jump in and "fix it" when a woman wants them to just listen—clearly the stereotype doesn't work in this case where they need to fix what's wrong. We need them to take what they see and hear and meet it with action.
>
> — Angie, a collabHERator

When Men Put Themselves in Our (High-Heeled) Shoes

Jeffery Tobias Halter, gender strategist, did just that—literally. During one of his presentations, he walked onstage wearing a pair of women's red pumps as a way to bring attention to what women face in the workplace. What makes this image so powerful is that it makes more real for men the issues that women face by putting a man in our shoes so that he might better imagine what we *feel*. In other words, if men were to walk even a mile in our shoes, how might they be transformed? How might they be better informed as to how to support us?

It reminds me of what facilitators know to be the case in the world of learning and development. People may not remember what you said in that training session, but they will remember how you made them feel. This tells us that the campaign to get more men onboard can't be carried out solely with rhetoric detailing the business case for gender equity. Again, it requires a *head* and *heart* approach that will lead to the joining together of *hands* for taking action.

Theresa M. Robinson

Misplaced Emphasis on Feeling and Understanding?

A head-heart-hands approach for gaining male allies generated much discussion with collabHERators. While we agree that more is needed beyond the business case approach where profit generation and innovation, for example, are emphasized, we disagree that the distinction between feeling and understanding versus accepting should not preclude men from becoming allies.

> **Get Real**
> It's not possible for men to feel what we feel or to understand what we experience. They can't because they are not us. I can't fully understand what it's like to be a man. I can try, but I can never fully understand. Instead of forcing men to feel and understand, the emphasis should be on acceptance. We don't want men to think that if they don't feel what we feel or understand what we experience as women, that they can't be allies or that they'll make lousy allies. What about accepting what women feel and accepting what women experience? Isn't that a better strategy?
>
> — Maya, a collabHERator

I find Maya's thoughts particularly striking, especially in light of my own experiences with my husband over the years. Going back to my example about my role in hiring a cleaner for our home, I have to say that there is something about my process that my husband has never understood, but has accepted after several rounds of dialogue.

If I am in town on our scheduled day of cleaning, I pre-clean my house before the cleaning lady arrives. I do this to minimize the potential perception that our home is dirty and disgusting. A more acceptable perception is that our home is only mildly dirty and slightly untidy, which wouldn't be a scathing indictment of my housekeeping skills.

My husband thinks I'm insane to clean the house right before paying someone else to do it. Though I've explained to him that I don't want the cleaning lady to think I'm dirty, HE DOESN'T UNDERSTAND. Though I've explained to him that I don't want the cleaning lady to think I don't know how to clean my own house, HE DOESN'T UNDERSTAND. Though I've explained to him that I care about what the cleaning lady thinks, HE DOESN'T UNDERSTAND.

It took several rounds of conversation for each of us to not understand each other. What came out of it though is that we finally accepted each other's perspective and have made it work. My husband doesn't need to understand my reasons why. Trying to understand was making both of us frustrated. Acceptance gave us peace and allowed us to move forward. More accurately, it was him realizing that backing off would restore balance, because in our household, if I ain't happy, ain't nobody happy!

Get Real

My husband decided it was easier for him to accept that I'd be scrubbing toilets on the morning of our scheduled cleaning day *if* I was home than for him to keep failing to understand why. I'm emphasizing the word *if* because one day my husband tried to catch me in a trap. On the date of our upcoming cleaning, I was scheduled to be away on a business trip. The day before my departure, he posed a question. "The cleaning lady will be here while you're

> gone. Are you planning to clean before your trip?" My response was, "No. Like you say, I won't be here when she comes. I don't care if she thinks you're dirty and filthy!"
> —Theresa, a collabHERator

Acceptance, not tolerance is key. Acceptance fosters respectful support. Tolerance lends itself to simmering resentment. My husband and I have embraced this philosophy even more in the last three years due to our son's autism spectrum disorder diagnosis. As he and I are neurotypical, there are just certain aspects of our son's thinking and behavior that we can't fully understand. That doesn't stop us from accepting his experiences, doesn't stop us from supporting him, and doesn't stop us from advocating on his behalf.

Men can be real allies for women when they accept our experiences. *I may not understand women and what they experience, but I care enough to accept their experiences, support their inclusion and belonging, and advocate for progress.*

As Maya stresses, a stronger focus on acceptance might be better. That's not to say that we should abandon *feel* and *understand* altogether. But think about the tension, frustration, and the misunderstanding we would avoid if we prioritized *acceptance* first. Think about the time we save when, instead of trying to convince men to *feel* and *understand*, we direct our efforts toward an approach to which they might more easily respond.

> **Get Real**
> Men don't feel. They respond.
> — Simone, a collabHERator

> **Get Real**
> Maybe we can be the catalyst for something that could happen. I realize we're not going to change that man's opinion unless we stop on the street, collect our emotions, not be aggressive, and say, "Listen, I know you probably meant well when you said that, but it's really offensive and this is why. I hope you have a good day. I'm gonna keep walking now, but don't say that again to a woman." I think men in general lack the awareness and empathy that women have, so they have to be trained.
> — Ashley, a collabHERator

Though the issues of inequity, discrimination, and injustice in this world are far more deep and complex to be highlighted by the symbolism of high-heeled shoes, it has taken generations of change for us to get this far in making a dent. But there is a choice that men can make. Men can choose to become more educated and aware of the issues. They can choose to work for change in our work environments and communities. They can choose compassion and understanding. Yes, I know. To show compassion is messy, inconvenient, and hard. My choice of compassion here means that I'm back to wanting men to understand...when it's possible, where there's capacity for it.

> **Get Real**
> Men miss the boat when their response is that they're hesitant to give a woman a compliment anymore, based on everything happening now. That's so ignorant.
> — Audrey, a collabHERator

> **Get Real**
> I really enjoy the company of the men I work with—just occasionally frustrated when I allow myself time to reflect on things that have been done and said during my career to date that shouldn't really have happened. Also frustrated by the lack of women in my industry in senior roles who I'd be able to bounce this kind of thing around with to know I'm not alone.
> — Cindy, a collabHERator

The "Only" Effect

How do you think a man would feel if he were the only man in a room full of women? I ask the question because it's not something I usually get to witness. Most times I'm the only woman or one of very few women in a room. Nearly two years ago, I had the opportunity to observe an "almost" situation. I was in a town outside of Amsterdam delivering a training session as part of a series for a group of leaders for a major pharmaceutical company.

For this division of the company, women comprised the majority. Each session in the series would accommodate up to thirty-six participants. As participants started trickling in for this particular session, I noticed that one table was still empty. And so far, all the participants were women. When the first male participant arrived, I noticed that once he signed the attendance roster, he turned to look at the room as if trying to decide where he should sit. Other than the one empty table, the other five had space for at least two more people. He decided to sit at the empty table.

Not even two minutes went by, when a second male entered the room. Upon scanning the room, he spotted the lone male at a table and joined him. The remainder of the participants to arrive were women. And though the table with the two men had the most available seats, none of the women chose to sit there. When everyone had taken their seats and the training started, five tables were exclusively women. And at one table, there sat two men and four empty chairs. Self-selected gender segregation.

I later discovered that the two men didn't really know each other prior to the training. When I asked them later in the day, out of curiosity, why they had chosen to sit separately at a table by themselves, one of them responded with a comment that was very telling, while the other one nodded his head in vigorous agreement.

"We don't like being outnumbered."

Yeah, it doesn't feel so good, does it? Welcome to our world, fellas. This is what many women feel like most of the time!

I could only smile, a smile that covered up a million more thoughts that remained unspoken.

> **Get Real**
> The household has been the realm of women for years and years, and the workplace was the realm of men. Work was their space, their kingdom. Then all of a sudden women started entering the workforce, and it wasn't men's space anymore. We were demanding to be hired, to participate, to be heard, to do this, to do that. Men didn't know how to handle all that. They still don't. The household is still the domain of women, but men don't have a domain anymore that's theirs.
> — Monica, a collabHERator

Monica's insights regarding "traditional" domains for women and "traditional" domains for men link to the role of the church in maintaining gender traditions. Just as there are differences in views on gender equity across home and the workplace, these differences can be exacerbated by and reinforced within the church.

Patrick, an advocate for women, found himself at the center of rigid views on gender roles held by the leadership team of his church. "I am a supporter of and advocate for women at my corporate job. I also serve at a large church as part of a teaching team that leads small groups of approximately forty people. One Sunday morning as I wrapped up the lesson for the group, I asked one of the women to close in prayer. She shook her head as if to say, 'No way!' When I brought this up two weeks later to the teaching team about having women pray in our small groups, the idea was met with resistance because it had never been done before in the more than ten years that the small groups have been in existence."

"I told the guys that I believed women should be allowed to lead prayers. I got immediately rejected. Two of the men thought it was inappropriate, and the third wasn't averse to the idea, but thought it would never fly. I let it go at the time. Men were against it, and the women didn't want to challenge the status quo and thus weren't willing to advocate as strongly."

"Later, I brought it up again when the new leaders rotated in. I told them the women should definitely be allowed to pray, and this time there was less resistance. One other fellow and I went ahead with it and invited the women to pray. Today, I don't think anyone is against women praying; it's just that they don't get called on as much. Though slow, it's progress."

Patrick's example illustrates several points: being an ally for women isn't a self-contained role within the walls of the job; women can be complicit in our own discrimination; gender challenges permeate every part of society. Specifically, what Patrick helps to further highlight is that men daily leave, what may be, their traditional households or leave their traditional churches and enter into the workplace where the gender rules are supposed to be different. Women are severely disadvantaged when men aren't able to make the transition or are unwilling to make the transition.

Women likewise may be leaving traditional roles at home or traditional roles and rules at church and entering into the workplace. Having compartmentalized multiples spaces and navigated multiple roles within those spaces, women are more capable of code-switching because we have to. Men aren't usually underrepresented or disempowered in spaces they occupy. Their empowerment is a constant.

Get Real

Here I am in the finance industry in 2018, and yet the same measuring stick continues to be used. If a woman raises her tone of voice in an office to highlight a point, she is aggressive. A man, however, saying the same thing is assertive. I could write so many examples of this stereotyping, but we all know what I am talking about. I once stopped a group of my fellow executives in their tracks. We were having drinks after a meeting and I arrived a little late. The guys were chatting away, oblivious to my presence. "My boiler's gone, but it's alright. The wife is waiting in for the plumber." "My wife is picking me up from the station tonight, so I can have a few drinks." "That reminds me. I must call my wife to pick up my dry cleaning." I said to the group, "This is fascinating. I must get myself one of those wife things."

> My frustration was that I would sacrifice everything in my homelife to be in the office, and there was no one to delegate my homelife to. In this world, if I had a husband he would be at work too, wouldn't he?
>
> — Cindy, a collabHERator

As Cindy points out, being the only woman on a team also means being the only woman at after-hours events and social gatherings, where the "only" status highlights even more the different experiences of women and men. What women face is not confined to nine to five, but extends to 24/7.

Brad from earlier admits that he's never been the only man among women but has perhaps come closest to the experience when he worked in human resources for a Native American tribe and its business units. "It was interesting, because more times than not, I felt like my thoughts or opinions were not taken seriously. I felt like I did not quite fit in. Even serious advice I provided to avoid adverse impact to their business was not always heeded. The bottom line was that I was brought in to do a job but did not feel valued because I was different. Quite the sobering experience and perspective. It also taught me to never treat someone like that and to be cognizant of the fact that someone else may feel the same way."

Ally Is a Verb

True allies that seek to elevate women and stop the unfair treatment say and do certain things. For one thing, allies ask, then truly listen. A prerequisite to listening is to stop talking—specifically, men must make a conscious decision to stop talking over women, overtalking women, and speaking for women. This doesn't mean that men will always get it right or that they won't make mistakes, but it's about modeling a sincere willingness to listen and a sincere desire to try.

> **Get Real**
> In a relationship, you can't keep trying to fix someone or always having to try to change someone to become the man that you need them to be. If we took that approach at work, men would get fired, versus we need to trust the process. The process is taking too long. Fire their asses, 'cause I'm done.
> — Simone, a collabHERator

My husband and I have attended various marriage retreats over the years and one of the most game-changing concepts that transformed our relationship is viewing love as a verb instead of a noun. That way the focus is on action. It's the same way with ally. If men just call themselves allies, they stay stuck in the being. And we clearly need them to do something! And when male allies join up with women, wholly committed and working together as a team, that's when change happens.

> **Get Real**
> Some men are idiots and will dig in their heels. No matter how many women come forward or how many similar stories we tell, some men won't believe us or change. Thank goodness there are men who do respond positively and believe us—men who are supportive and are doing something.
> — Dawn, a collabHERator

Speaking of doing, being an ally is an ongoing commitment. Women don't get to take a break from being women. We don't get a break from experiencing discrimination, misogyny, sexism, abuse, assaults, etc. Women want allies to work just as hard as we do for change.

Doug, an internal consultant, is a strong proponent of male allies working intentionally to offer themselves as honest resources in situations where they can help women. The example he shares is evidence that mentorship and support should be an equal opportunity across gender. "My company had gone through a massive restructuring and was being transitioned to new leadership. I had a choice to either help the new leader transition smoothly or to step away from the situation entirely. Once I discovered the new leader was a woman who I had originally been a part of hiring, I was thrilled and wanted to do everything I could to set her up for success."

"My original meeting with her lasted for about three hours. I focused on listening to her ideas and concerns coming into the new group. During the critically important and transparent conversation, I was able to speak to some of her concerns and validate some of the more difficult aspects of the transition."

"Over the next several weeks of the transition, she and I met and debriefed frequently. I wanted to ensure her that I was available as a support resource for what questions she might have. I also met with the team she was inheriting, who were not expecting a leader shift and had no prior interaction with her. I met with them individually to talk through the change and also to express my endorsement of her strengths."

"Once the transition period had progressed further, and the leader was more settled in her new responsibilities,

I made sure to let her know how well I thought she was doing. I also let others know. And it was true. She took several initiatives to the next level, making them more productive and more efficient."

In following Doug's account, I noticed that his support of the new leader was a series of actionable steps. He listened to her, he set up regular meetings with her, he intervened on her behalf with the team she was inheriting, he recognized her for her accomplishments, and he communicated her accomplishments to others. Doug's support of her was not dependent on him needing to understand what she may have been feeling or experiencing. Who's to say that this element was not a part of their conversations. In the end though, his support was practical and actionable, and it worked.

That One Time Doesn't Make Men Allies

Lest we think the accounts from male allies in this chapter represent single instances, these men are part of a group of men that are out there consistently working on behalf of women in their sphere of influence. These men exhibit consistent behaviors in their lives that support and value women. And as Patrick shows, it's not just what they do inside the workplace, it's also how they show up outside of work. Not all of them have daughters, as fatherhood is not an ally requirement.

We should be careful to not share their "one story" with other men in such a way that they misinterpret it as proof of one's ally status. It may take only one behavior for a man to be labelled asshole, but it takes more than one behavior for him to earn his ally card. In other words, just as I don't care to be touted to others as your one black woman friend, women don't appreciate a man telling others that he's an ally for women because of that one time two years ago when he got his neighbor's daughter an internship at his company. True ally? Nope. We see right through that.

Teaching Old Dogs New Tricks

Several collabHERators believe that men who are rigid and knowingly perpetuate gender inequity are a waste of effort if we are looking for change now. It will be the men with a heart for fairness who just need a nudge into action, that can make the biggest difference and most immediate impact.

> **Get Real**
> In any area of our lives or in any organization there are going to be men who just want things a certain way, and they're not going to change. So, the key isn't whether or not we can change them. The key is so how do we work around them and still accomplish change.
> — Priscilla, a collabHERator

Reach one, teach one. And so on and so on. Men with a clue have a responsibility to enlighten clueless men. Critical mass has not been reached yet, and so we have to keep it going. One man or a few men cannot expect to do it without organized critical mass.

> **Get Real**
> I get it now. With the Black Lives Matter movement, I was quick to chime in as a white person with the response, "all lives matter." I understand now that the movement is about bringing change through greater awareness that black lives aren't being valued and not that black lives matter more than any other group. As a survivor of sexual

> assault and sexual harassment in the workplace, the "#MeToo and #TimesUp movements represent acknowledgment of what I experienced. The aim is to stop the assault and harassment of women. So, when I hear the #NotAllMen response, I am angry that there are those out there that think there was ever the implication that all men harass and assault women. Duh! Of course, we know it's not all men! And to say it in response to #MeToo and #TimesUp is downright insensitive to women who've been victimized and takes away from stopping the behaviors of the horrible men that are the focus of the movements. #NotAllMen makes women who've been preyed upon and victimized feel like they're complaining and should remain silent about these behaviors, so we can cheer for men. Men don't deserve a fucking medal because they don't rape or harass women! It's called normal decent behavior! So, stop with all the #NotAllMen and let women finally tell their stories and let change happen where it needs to!
>
> — Joni, a collabHERator

Yes, many men (and women) are quick to say #NotAllMen. Good men do exist. Male allies and advocates are out there, but even they can unconsciously perpetuate gender stereotypes that make them complicit. They can't be exempt from ongoing re-educating. Joni is right. When we pronounce that not all men engage in sexist and misogynistic behaviors, we have to be mindful of striking a balance that does not elevate "good men" at the expense of victims of such behaviors, who have bravely come forward with their stories.

The Rule of Opposites

When I served as a diversity and inclusion consultant for Disney, there was a rule that a person of color had to always have a white cofacilitator, that a woman always had to have a male cofacilitator, that a person with a disability always had to have an able-bodied cofacilitator. And so on. You get the idea. It's the same reasoning behind why it's so critical for men to step up to not only end gender inequity, but also to advance women. Real change happens when men speak up and stand up, especially white men, the dominant group that has historically been in power. When men hear from men, it's extremely powerful and compelling.

> **Get Real**
> Having mothers, wives, girlfriends, daughters, and sisters hasn't done the trick. Men need women mentors who will take them from asshole behavior to ally behavior.
> — Margaret, a collabHERator

Man Up

Not only do men need to be willing to listen to female voices, they have a responsibility to listen. To not listen is to let our differences control us, divide us, and paralyze us. When men listen, truly listen, it creates an opportunity to forge deeper connections and deeper relationships that lead to better ways to work together and coexist. Win win.

> **Get Real**
> I know that there are people out there that think #MeToo and #TimesUp have become a witch hunt. Maybe there is some of that in some places, but you know what, I just

> hope men are evaluating their behavior. And what I want for women is for us to turn this into a focus on empowerment.
>
> — Deirdre, a collabHERator

Be UncomMEN

Valuing gender equity and inclusion is a great start. However, it's ultimately behavior that makes it real. It's about moving from mindset to skillset. If men truly want to foster gender equity and advocate for the advancement of women, they should pay attention to women who make them uncomfortable and figure out why. They should also pay attention to how they respond to women: particularly those who contradict their assumptions, ones they don't like, ones they don't understand, and ones with whom they don't work well.

> **Get Real**
>
> Men are more conscious now thanks to thousands of women. I think it's gonna border on an epidemic with this situation we're having right now. Women who have been marginalized, abused, or disrespected, but didn't have the courage to speak out until one brave person came forward. Now we're all coming forward. The sex piece of it is the first tear to the fabric. There's a lot more around the relations between men and women than just the sexual assault piece. It was the opening tears or the first phase.
>
> — Britney, a collabHERator

Amen for Some Men

Not every clueless and action-less man will necessarily remain so. And our alliances with them are worth forging. Alliances that are worth it to leave our stubborn and wounded isolation and join with them. Worth it to forgive and forget betraying women. Worth it to give our time and energy to mentoring. Worth it to push through the discomfort and messiness of being in relationship. Worth it to seek to understand and be understood. Worth it to extend acceptance, when understanding eludes us.

We need allies who will speak out on our behalf, help to rightfully advance us, stand up and stand out for us, advise us, coach us, mentor us, get to know us, accept us.

**Not Every Man is Clueless and Action-less…
Get Over It!
Tips and Strategies for Encouraging Men to
Support Women**

1. Invite a male friend or colleague to an event that promotes women's interests.

2. Publicly commend the ideas and achievements of women to others.

3. Seek to be mentored and be a mentor to men.

4. Host a lunch-and-learn and invite women and men.

5. Enlist male colleagues in creating safe spaces for women to be heard.

6. Challenge men in the workplace to take the Male Advocacy Profile quiz at http://ywomen.biz/male-advocacy-profile/#survey .

7. Lobby to get *Gender Conversation Quickstarter* on the meeting agenda.

8. Share with a male colleague a story that personalizes gender disparity.

9. Ask a male colleague to write a commendation letter for your files.

10. Ask men to join a workplace task force to create women-friendly policies.

Reflection Questions

1. How have you, knowingly or unknowingly, blamed all men as "the enemy?"
2. Where have you been intentional about forging alliances with men at work?
3. What men make potential good allies and why?

* * *

Do-Over Challenge

Some allies are hiding in plain sight just waiting to be activated. Some of them have revealed small clues indicating that they would be great supporters if they knew what to do.

You deserve a do-over. Take a second look at the men in your work environment. Find at least three men who, with some coaching, would be good allies for women.

Write their names on the lines below and commit to beginning ally onboarding within the next four weeks.

Ally potential #1: _____

Ally potential #2: _____

Ally potential #3: _____

Make-Over Challenge

Challenge your male partner, a male colleague, a male family member, or a male friend to predict where he falls on the Male Ally Continuum. Here are the five categories, in ascending ranking order on the continuum, from one to five.

Unaware
Understanding
Ally
Champion
Advocate

Once he makes the prediction, have him then go to the YWomen website to take the Male Advocacy Profile quiz, a series of twenty questions.

http://ywomen.biz/male-advocacy-profile/#survey

The results from the quiz will provide him with a description of the category in which he fits and will provide tips and actions to champion and advocate for women.

Theresa M. Robinson

Conclusion

We realize the importance of our voices only when we are silenced."

— Malala Yousafzai

As we enter this last chapter of this part of the journey, I have good news and bad news. Which do you want to hear first? Okay, here's the bad news. When you finish reading this book, there may not have been a single thing that has changed out there for you. All the tiring, unfair crap is still there. It's all still there.

It's Not Fair

Being a woman can be tough—whether in our roles as partner, mother, or leader and influencer in the workplace. But especially in the workplace. Despite gender inequities in behaviors, opportunities, and pay, we attempt to manage our lives outside of work, all the while trying to tend to our health and well-being.

Outside of work, with family and friends, we're more willing to be authentically messy in our relationships. For example, Jessica can tell her husband to stop saying that he's babysitting their kids when she's at yoga class. She can even call him a moron, while explaining to him that fathers don't babysit their own kids. And she can point out that nobody—male or female—refers to a mother spending time with her kids as babysitting.

And Sasha can explain to her young kids that mommies can be engineers, and daddies can cook dinner. She can also clarify for them that she is washing the dishes not because doing so is "woman's work," but because she's sharing the workload with daddy who cooked dinner.

I can cut right to the chase with my husband and call him stupid or a dumbass, because we've already laid the groundwork and had the messy, uncomfortable conversations. He has his own history of internalizing gender messages and conditioning. We work together in our relationship to unlearn them together.

Things are not so in the workplace. What do we do about it at work when others doubt our abilities or put us down based on their ideas of how we should act or what our role should be? What if we've heard it outright a woman described as "bossy?" And what of those times we've witnessed a woman put forth an idea, only to be ignored, while a man puts forth the same idea and is praised?

Yes, it's not fair. We agree on that.
Clench your teeth.
Ball up your fists.
Scream.
Yell.
Be "unladylike."
Now what?
Nevertheless, she persisted.
Take a deep cleansing breath.
Gather yourself.
Come close. I want to be sure you get this.

Know your power source. Jane, divorced mother of two, referred earlier to hers as her inner goddess. (Beyonce refers to hers as Sasha Fierce). If you've done exercises in the book, you know your power source. Deep down you've always had it. Access it and stay plugged in.

> **Get Real**
> No, we're not going to change the world around us overnight. No, we're not going to change the companies we work for overnight. And no, there will be some things and some people that simply will not change. The beautiful thing about change is that I always have control over changing me, control over changing things I can do for me.
> — Dominique, a collabHERator

The Light of Our Power Source

Now the good news. *There may not have been a single thing that has changed out there.* On the face of it, it looks to be identical to the previously stated bad news. However, if you don't study it closely, you'll miss it and think that the good news matches the bad news. Look again. This time, I'll make it easier for you. There may not have been a single thing that has changed *out* there. Did you catch it this time? Do you get it? What we have control over isn't *out* there. It's *in* here. Within ourselves. Have you felt a shift within from reading the stories and engaging with the exercises? Transformation doesn't require a change in our circumstances. That's why it's important that each of us knows our power source.

> **Get Real**
> When I have a plan and set dates for different stages of the plan, that motivates me. The minute I have that final end date, I can see the light at the end of the tunnel. It motivates me. It's when I can actually create the beginning of a transformation because I only have to hang in there for a specified predetermined amount of time. It's what you explained about vacation. When people know their vacation is coming up, all of a sudden, they get these bursts of energy and they're productive and happy. They see the end! Hallelujah!
> — Katherine, a collabHERator

> **Get Real**
> I have days when I'm firing mad that I have to deal with the bullshit another day. I have moments when I want to say, "fuck it" and walk out. I also have periods when I decide to just suck it up and then complain and vent to anybody who'll listen.
> — Kim, a collabHERator

Pursuing a Full-Out Life

What is a full-out life? Cassie, a career transition architect, has some ideas on that. "Living a full-out life means not living with regrets. It means living as if today is my last day. I want to be able to say 'wow' about who I am and what I've done without thinking on who I could have been or what I could have done. Living full-out is knowing I've given the best of me to the world, and I challenged myself every day to be joyful and to live in love instead of fear."

Many collabHERators expressed sentiments similar to Cassie's while using different words. It's another element that draws all of us together collectively. At the same time, there were practical concerns expressed about whether a full-out life for women is compatible with the current state of things. In other words, how can women pursue their vision of a full-out life despite so much work still needing to be done around gender equity and inclusion?

Sometimes the primary blocker of the pursuit of what we want ends up being in our own heads. It's limitations we may be putting on ourselves while projecting them onto external challenges. According to Cassie, the key to pursuing anything is small steps. "For overachievers and high achievers, it can be incredibly humbling to think in terms of small steps, especially those of us who have achieved great success. Many of us who have made it to the top of one mountain can look over to another peak and be determined to get there. But we can't go from peak to peak without first coming down from the mountain we're on and starting at the bottom of the next mountain. It's how we reach the top again. It's steps."

"That's when some of us begin to over rationalize. We think in terms of whether we have the strength and flexibility. Maybe we think about changing the lifestyle to which we're accustomed. Then we conclude that this is going to be really tough."

"That kind of thinking is bullshit. Excuses. They're all excuses, and I've made plenty of them in my life. What I found is that the more self-awareness I lack, and the more successful I get, and the more self- involved I get, then the sneakier I get about the excuses I make. I get sneakier because there are always good reasons to not pursue something. It's scary. It's risky. I'll be vulnerable. There are all kinds of excuses, but even the logical ones won't make sense if I know in my heart that I have to come down from that comfortable mountain and have the gumption to climb another one. So, small steps are a big thing for me."

Cassie refers to a phenomenon that she calls the dark side of personal development, self-empowerment, and change. "We all want to sit and talk about that other mountain and all of our dreams, our hopes, and all the things we could achieve. That's all awesome and a great place to start because there should be a lot of time spent on that. But examining how we are holding our own self back and why we're making excuses—that's the real depth. Exploring the fears we have is important. If we equate happiness with freedom, what does that mean? Why do we care so much about what people think who don't matter? How do we get untangled from the political games that people play? All of this is within us to be explored."

We're all marked by challenges that make us strong not because we escaped them, but because we persevered through them, overcame them. Each of us is more than the circumstances of what's been said to us or done to us. It's our wholeness and not our treatment that defines us. That gender inequities don't define us is determined by the high value and worthiness we assign to ourselves.

I'm being very conservative here. Yet consider that every woman at least once in her lifetime will experience some form of gender bias and discrimination. What this means is that we're not alone in what we experience no matter how alone we feel. We can surround ourselves with others who know and understand. We can share our stories, our strategies, and our successes. We can find strength and comfort and be a part of the tremendous tribal support of women.

The beginning of our new narrative starts with developing and nurturing warrior-like strength, endurance, and resilience in response to the unfair or the unexpected. We can then feel empowered to speak up for what we need with a courageous voice that seeks out what we need and won't settle for less. And when we're judged for our outward appearance, we can dismiss those imposed gender standards of superficiality in favor of our inner self where our values, beliefs, and inner convictions live. When we know and acknowledge our inner beauty and inner uniqueness, we don't care anymore what other people think of us. When we encounter personal roadblocks we get to practice bulldozing barriers or designing our own detours and then sharing the way with others. When our sleep is threatened by anxiety, we get to dream while we're still awake and never give up.

How powerful we are when we live from our source. How tall we are when we rise up from the shadows of misplaced expectations, imposed invisibility, and unfair treatment to say out loud what needs to be said.

Get Real
I'm not quiet and demure; I don't conform. I also look and act differently. I am being who I know to be—myself. That's my superpower.

— Toni, a collabHERator

Strong Is the New Beautiful

Raising our voice is not about getting loud or disagreeing for the sake of disagreeing. It is about recognizing that our voice matters and can take us farther than we thought possible. When we overcome the limitations placed on us by others, that's one type of victory. And when we rise up and overcome the limitation we place on ourselves, that's when we truly develop inner strength and fortitude.

We need to keep telling and hearing our own stories. In our communal sharing, we grow stronger together. And when we act from a place of strength, change happens. When we live this open, transparent, beautifully broken life, we understand who we have always been.

> ### Get Real
> We women have to share our stories as a way to empower us to take the next step. It's important to start speaking and sharing our stories because one woman's story may be just the motivation another woman needs to act on something in her own life. It can provide hope. For me, sharing my story also holds me accountable to me. I can't play chicken anymore.
> — Victoria, a collabHERator

What is the next step? This, our book, with its stories, tactics and advice lays the foundation for a stronger movement. I turn it over to you to go out and promote the change you feel within—powered by your source and activated by your experiences with make-overs and do-overs.

This book is a start. With the talent and skill you possess, how can you join up and connect with others?

Though my collabHERators' identities I've promised to keep confidential so as to not risk potential negative ramifications at their places of work, they and you are out there. Let's find each other. That is my call to action for each and every one of us.

We are stronger than we know. And we can take control of our life.

Strength and resilience are what we've possessed all along. We just need to be reactivated from time to time. Because we've endured so much over our lifetime in the way of injustices, inequities, sexism, discrimination, etc., life can start to feel like an either-or proposition. Persevere or crumble. Bounce back or die.

Every time one of us beats the system, the brokenness of the system is highlighted and exposed. It takes one voice to make it a little bit harder the next time for that jerk. And we won't stop until we completely dismantle the system that allows him to say or do something in the first place.

And every time one of us takes measures to ensure that we are well in mind, body, and spirit, it serves as an example to other women of what's possible when we prioritize our well-being.

Even when we don't individually have it all together all of the time, we're still better together.

Are we there yet?

No, we're not there yet. It's going to be a journey to get there.

Are we there yet?

We'll get there by enduring with one another and bearing with one another.

Are we there yet?

Theresa M. Robinson

We'll get there by doing life together and telling our stories to ourselves while simultaneously releasing them to the world with courage and hope, one story at a time. What matters the most is not how far we have to go, but that we continue in the right direction.

It's a collective journey. We cannot stop. We will not stop.

Ready to link arms, put on the full armor, and journey on together?

We've still got a long way to go, baby.
Things are better, but not yet right.
But, connected to our source, we got this!

Invitation to CollabHERate

We invite you to continue your experience with *Women Overcoming O-Syndrome*:

- Share your experiences, get guidance and support, and connect with women in the LinkedIn group, *Women Overcoming O-Syndrome*. For an invitation, please send your request to myvoice@Osyndrome.com or message Theresa M. Robinson on LinkedIn.
- Communicate with Theresa by sending a message to myvoice@Osyndrome.com.

If you found value in *Women Overcoming O-Syndrome*, please consider these ideas for passing it on and continuing the momentum needed for real change:

- Buy ten copies and give them to those you think this book will help.

- Choose this book for an upcoming book club meeting.
- Use this book as a gift for your team members at work.
- In addition to joining the LinkedIn group, create a small support group of collabHERators.
- Post your comments about the book on Amazon.

For information on having Theresa speak at your organization or team event, please inquire at info@mastertrainertmr.com.

Also by Author

O-Syndrome: When Work is 24/7 and You're Not

About the Authors

Theresa M. Robinson is the founder and president of Master Trainer TMR & Associates, a training consulting firm. In her work with busy professionals, it became clear to her that many were echoing the same sentiment – that "work is 24/7, but I'm not"—leading to feelings of overwhelm and overload. Giving voice to the phenomenon that she terms O-Syndrome, Theresa has dedicated her career to providing insights and practical strategies for navigating our professional and personal lives. An ATD Master Trainer and an outspoken advocate with over 25 years of experience, she coaches and advises working professionals all over the world in the areas of pressures, priorities, and purpose. Based in Houston, TX, she is currently working on her third book which focuses on relationship strategies in the digital age for busy professionals, debuting summer 2019.

CollabHERators™: crazy brave, fiercely resilient, stereotype-busting, insanely courageous, relentlessly determined, wildly successful women.

Contact Theresa M. Robinson

Well-Being & Inclusion Catalyst / Facilitator / Speaker / Coach / Author

To reach **Theresa M. Robinson,** regarding speaking engagements, training facilitation, coaching, upcoming seminars and conferences, or to read about her upcoming books, articles and posts, please visit her @

www.TheresaMRobinson.com

Speaking & Workshop Topics include:
Leadership
Wellness
Work-Life Balance
Life Strategies for Women
Diversity and Inclusion
Team Building

www.ingramcontent.com/pod-product-compliance
Lightning Source LLC
Chambersburg PA
CBHW070532010526
44118CB00012B/1112